M000275935

What Others Are Saying about Bishop Henry Fernandez and *Favor Unleashed*

"Sometimes the easiest thing to say is the hardest thing to believe. Most of us have no problem saying we're blessed, but living like we actually believe it is an entirely different thing. In *Favor Unleashed*, Henry Fernandez shows how God desires for each of us to live a life that's ultimately narrated by His grace."

—*Steven Furtick*
Pastor, Elevation Church
New York Times best-selling author

"Bishop Henry B. Fernandez is a dedicated spiritual leader in our community. He strives to empower others through his generosity and support. I truly appreciate the positive difference he makes in the lives of so many each and every day."

—*Marty Kiar*
Broward County Property Appraiser
Fort Lauderdale, FL

"*Favor Unleashed* will transform your life! Bishop Fernandez's deep passion for faith will inspire you to take action. This book will activate your faith, encourage your heart, and stir your soul to victory!"

—*Dr. Traci Lynn*
CEO and founder, Traci Lynn Jewelry

FAVOR
UNLEASHED

HENRY FERNANDEZ

WHITAKER
HOUSE

FAVOR UNLEASHED:
EMBRACING GOD'S BEST FOR YOU

HenryFernandezMinistries.org
information@henryfernandez.org

ISBN: 978-1-62911-882-6
eBook ISBN: 978-1-62911-883-3
Printed in the United States of America
© 2017 by Henry Fernandez

Whitaker House
1030 Hunt Valley Circle
New Kensington, PA 15068
www.whitakerhouse.com

Library of Congress Cataloging-in-Publication Data
Names: Fernandez, Henry, 1964- author.
Title: Favor unleashed : embracing God's best for you / by Henry Fernandez.
Description: New Kensington, PA : Whitaker House, 2017. |
Identifiers: LCCN 2017027932 (print) | LCCN 2017031682 (ebook) | ISBN
   9781629118833 (ebook) | ISBN 9781629118826 (trade pbk. : alk. paper)
Subjects: LCSH: God (Christianity)--Promises.
Classification: LCC BT180.P7 (ebook) | LCC BT180.P7 F47 2017 (print) | DDC
   248.4--dc23
LC record available at https://lccn.loc.gov/2017027932

1 2 3 4 5 6 7 8 9 10 11 ⑭ 24 23 22 21 20 19 18 17

DEDICATION

This book is dedicated to every individual who is seeking to fulfill his or her destiny. Yes, this book is dedicated to YOU! Deep inside every person, the loving heavenly Father has placed a passion to succeed—to attain everything for which He created us. Although each of us face challenges and obstacles in life, along with many responsibilities that compete for our attention, God has also given each of us the spirit of a warrior that compels us to "fight the good fight" in front of us until we embrace all that He has ordained for us.

I dedicate this book to you because you are such a person. Over the past twenty-five years I have had the joy of helping many people just like you discover and embrace God's destiny and purpose for their lives. It is individuals like you who inspire and motivate me, because I know the good plan He has for you. He loves you completely, He has delivered you from all your sin and failures—even those you're still struggling with—and He stands ready to chase you down with blessings, prosperity, and purpose for every area of your life. May God richly bless you as you step into His unfolding, perfect plan!

CONTENTS

FOREWORD

Favor Unleashed: Embracing God's Best for You is a rare combination of biblical insight and catalytic personal development. It contains the proof that God does not want to withhold anything from you but rather wants to load you to capacity with benefits through discovering the dimension of favor.

Gaining an understanding of the phenomenon of favor has the power to quantum-leap your life and empower you to significantly impact the world! Throughout history, we can see that those who had favor on their lives made the greatest impact on society and excelled in ways that would not have been otherwise possible.

In my own life, favor has been the indispensable key that has opened countless doors of opportunity for me to fulfill my destiny in shaping the trajectory of economies and nations.

I am so thankful that my dear friend Bishop Henry Fernandez has written this important book about how to unleash the power of God's favor in our lives. He is well qualified and intimately acquainted with this dimension of unmerited blessing and unusual grace. I have personally witnessed divine favor upon his life and I believe that there is a supernatural transference for you within the pages of this book as you devour its contents.

Every Christian book fills a vital role. However, *this* one is a masterpiece in preparing generations to reside in a unique dimension for a mission that goes far beyond the average mandate.

Presented within these pages is a gushing geyser of truth that has the potential to ignite your dreams to flourish as you encounter the power of favor. If, in the pursuit of your dreams, you've felt stuck, restless, discouraged, not good enough, or disqualified, then this book is for you, as those are only indications that you have outgrown your present reality and you're ready to enter the often discounted, but extremely potent, dimension of favor. Bishop Henry Fernandez eloquently takes the concept of favor to places it has never been before so that you can go to places you have never gone before.

Prepare to receive enlightenment. Prepare to receive practical insights that will forever change your life—prepare to receive favor!

—*Dr. Cindy Trimm*
Founder, Cindy Trimm Ministries
International conference host and speaker
Bestselling author of *Commanding Your Morning,*
Prevail, and over forty other titles
www.cindytrimm.com

INTRODUCTION:
YOU WERE CREATED FOR SUCCESS!

I want to start this book off right away with a little secret:

You are blessed.

That's right! In the here and now, in every area of your life, you are highly favored. Almighty God—the source of all blessings and good that comes to any of us—has deposited in your heavenly account everything you need to succeed and prosper beyond your wildest expectations.

All the dreams that you have held so deeply in your heart for many years, the ones that you may have given up on long ago as unattainable, are still in active mode, waiting for you like a trusted friend. The plans, expectations, goals, and ambitions from your past that may have faded into dim memories—those that are God-inspired, prophetic, and etched into your very soul—have the same power and potential as when the heavenly Father first dropped them into your spirit.

Yes, if I know anything about how the kingdom of God operates, I know this with certainty: You are blessed!

> **IF I KNOW ANYTHING ABOUT HOW THE KINGDOM OF GOD OPERATES, I KNOW THIS WITH CERTAINTY: YOU ARE BLESSED!**

EVERYONE FACES ADVERSITY

Now, you may think that these are easy words for me to say, something I am tossing off casually in an effort to help people who are struggling in life to feel better about themselves. Perhaps the reality of your own circumstances seems to be proof of anything *but* God's abundant blessing. Maybe, like so many people today, you are struggling financially, physically, or emotionally; maybe you're stuck in a job you hate or maybe you feel paralyzed in a dead-end position. Maybe you're suffering through the effects of a broken marriage or a relationship that has ended, or maybe you're heartbroken over a child who has made some poor choices.

Every person, at some point in life, faces hardships and trials. When we're in over our heads in the tides of life that pound against every single one of us, it can be easy to slide into hopelessness and despair, to begin to think that things will never change, to assume we'll never find the place of destiny and success that every person craves. *I'll never get out of debt. I'll never find where I fit in life. I'll never finish school and find a good job. I'll never be healed. I'll never find that significant someone to share my life with.*

The variations of "I'll never," "I can't," and "It will never happen" that our minds throw at us are endless, and each self-prophecy of failure and defeat seems to plunge us deeper into despair.

THE POWER OF GOD'S GRACE

I want to tell you from personal experience that if you find yourself in such a mode of thinking or with such an attitude, then you aren't counting on the most powerful resource known to humanity—a power that is even now available to you, right this second: God's unending grace. "But what is grace?" you might be asking. "I've heard the word, and I know it's supposed to be something good that God has for me. But what is it, really, and how can it possibly make a difference in my life?"

Two simple but divinely powered words will answer your questions: *unmerited favor*. Those two words make all the difference between failure and success. Those two words indicate God's desire to do you good despite your unworthiness and your absolute inability to help out. You can't gain God's grace by your own efforts, you can't increase its flow in your life by trying a little harder. In fact, just the opposite is true. Our own ham-handed efforts to "help God out" in guiding our lives inevitably land us in a world of trouble and grief.

> **OUR OWN HAM-HANDED EFFORTS TO "HELP GOD OUT" IN GUIDING OUR LIVES INEVITABLY LAND US IN A WORLD OF TROUBLE AND GRIEF.**

The problem is that while many of God's people today acknowledge the *concept* of grace—that they are saved from their sins through the death and resurrection of Jesus Christ—they really don't understand the *power* of God's grace—His unmerited favor—to give them success and victory in every area of their lives. God tells us in His Word that He is willing, able, and ready, through Jesus Christ, to meet all of our needs out of His unlimited storehouse of riches.[1] We are the King's kids and He has given us open access to His heavenly account which we can draw on at any time!

---

1. See Philippians 4:19.

WE ARE THE KING'S KIDS AND HE HAS GIVEN US OPEN ACCESS TO HIS HEAVENLY ACCOUNT WHICH WE CAN DRAW ON AT ANY TIME!

A PRODIGAL MENTALITY

The Christians who live out their days as if their heavenly Father is reluctant to give them anything are like the Prodigal Son. Jesus tells the story in Luke 15 of this young man who left the home of his wealthy and generous father and wasted all of his inheritance on drunken, foolish living. When he came to his senses and decided to return to his father, this unworthy son came home with the full expectation of living the remainder of his days as a mere slave in his father's house. It wasn't until he was confronted with the full force of his father's deep compassion toward him, of his father's great love for him despite his failures and the pain he had caused, that the Prodigal Son understood his father had received him back as though he had never left.

I am reminded of an old story about a man who, in his youth, left a loving home and community where his father was a well-known, wealthy, and highly respected businessman. After years adventuring around the country and wasting his life and opportunities on worthless pursuits, the man one day found himself back in the city where he had grown up, a hopeless, broken wreck living on whatever he could beg from passersby on the street.

Ashamed of being recognized as the no-good son who broke his mother's heart, sullied his father's good name, and threw away his fortune and future, the man crept around town for months bumming a dollar here and a meal there from those he was sure wouldn't know him. One day in a crowd he touched a stranger on the shoulder and asked in a shaky voice, "Sir, could you spare a dollar to help me get something to eat?" As the stranger turned around, the man was shocked to look into the face of his own father, who immediately recognized his long-lost boy and threw his arms around him. "My son!" he cried, "I've finally found you. A dollar, you say? Don't you realize that all I have is yours and I've been waiting for you to return? Welcome home!"

ARE YOU MISSING SOMETHING?

Are you like that broken-down man today? Have you lost sight of the wondrous riches of God's inheritance for you, bought and paid for by the blood of Jesus Christ? Have years of wandering, wounding, brokenness, and despair left you blind to the reality of who you are and the authority that is yours through Christ? Have you lost the hope of tomorrow, the assurance of a rich destiny that is the treasure of every true child of God? Is the grace of God—the unmerited favor that He promised for you—nothing more than a meaningless word?

Maybe the above scenario is not where you're at. Perhaps you're doing just fine in life, with a good job and income, a comfortable lifestyle, a great home and family. Maybe by all the measurements the world uses, you are a success. Still, I'd be willing to bet, there's a nagging doubt somewhere deep inside you that no one else can really see. For all that you've accomplished, for all the accolades, prestige, and esteem of others, there is an emptiness and dissatisfaction that you just can't shake. As you take stock of your past and reflect on your future, you're wondering if you've missed out on something important. What's that all about? Is there more to life than you've built by your own efforts?

Or maybe you're wondering what would happen if you woke up one morning to find yourself losing the things you value. What if your company downsizes and you suddenly find yourself looking for a new job? Or what if the business you've taken years of sweat and toil to build into a successful venture begins losing momentum, the valued customers slowly disappearing? What if a simple visit to the doctor for your annual physical reveals a life-threatening ailment? What if you lose a loved one who means the world to you?

What if, in the saddest scenario of all, nothing changes and you come to the end of your life having succeeded financially, relationally, and in every other earthly sphere—but have nothing of eternal value to show for all the years of life you lived? What if, as Jesus put it, you gain the whole world but lose your soul?[2]

REACHING HIGHER

The truth of the matter is that whether you are living at a high level of success and accomplishment and have found a fair degree of personal satisfaction in life or you are struggling in any of a number of areas to find your place and purpose, the Creator of the universe and our heavenly Father has so much more for each of us than meets the eye.

Yes, that includes the financial favor necessary to meet our needs and those of our family and loved ones; a job, career, or calling that is meaningful and lines up with our abilities and interests; and successful, fulfilling relationships that don't hurt us emotionally. God has a destiny in the here and now for each of us with success, victory, and peace written all over it.

But there is more.

Part and parcel of all that success is something that can't be measured with financial security, a satisfying vocation, solid relationships, or anything else this world can give. That *something* is really some-one—Jesus—who said that He came so that each of us might have joy and satisfaction in every area of life. For those of you who know the story of Jesus—how He came as God's Son, lived, died, and rose again—you realize that His promise of abundance and blessing in every corner of our lives cost Him everything He had.

2. See Matthew 16:26.

This book is all about showing you how you can access the abundance that Jesus Christ purchased for you on the cross of Calvary, and how you can live in that abundance every day for the rest of your life. If the abundance you need right now means improved finances, a better education and a career or job move, healing in your body, and restored and renewed relationships, take heart, you are on the right path.

Or if that abundance you seek tends more toward a renewal inside yourself, a peace of mind and heart, a closer relationship with God, and a life that will matter for all eternity, again, you have come to the right place!

Stay tuned and read on, because every chapter is packed with inspiring and motivational stories, simple godly counsel, and challenging advice that will help you move up to the next level of God's destiny for you.

1

THE SEEDS OF TRUE GREATNESS

I am the greatest!"

It's not difficult to remember who made those famed words his bold calling card throughout a storied athletic career. Cassius Clay, destined to become known to the world as legendary heavyweight boxing champion Muhammad Ali, first declared himself to be the "greatest" before his February 25, 1964, bout with then-heavyweight-champion Sonny Liston. Considered outmatched in nearly every department by the notoriously hard-hitting, ruthless, and far more experienced Liston, the twenty-two-year-old newcomer to professional boxing was making quite a prediction when he guaranteed to newspaper reporters that Liston would "fall in eight to prove that I'm great."[1]

But when newcomer Muhammad Ali, a long-shot seven-to-one underdog in the fight, easily stopped Liston after only six rounds, sports reporters and fight fans began to wonder if the brash young boxer might know something about his ability that they had missed. And, indeed, over the next several years, as he felled a long list of

---

1. Muhammad Ali, quoted in Thomas Hauser, *Muhammad Ali: His Life and Times* (New York, Simon and Schuster, 1992), 61.

worthy opponents to become the only three-time heavyweight champion in history, Muhammad Ali proved that his words went beyond mere bragging by going down in history as the "greatest" boxer of all time.

EVERYONE WANTS GREATNESS

Believe it or not, what Muhammad Ali said goes to the very heart of something that dwells deep inside every person: the need for greatness. That's right. If you look closely you will find in every human being the desire to excel, to be the best we can be, to be at the top of our game—in short, to be great.

> IF YOU LOOK CLOSELY YOU WILL FIND IN EVERY HUMAN BEING THE DESIRE TO EXCEL, TO BE THE BEST WE CAN BE, TO BE AT THE TOP OF OUR GAME—IN SHORT, TO BE GREAT.

From the homeless person on the street and the nameless face in the crowd, to kings, presidents, financial giants, and those whose names have become synonymous with some incredible achievement, every person, if he or she were honest, would admit that they are motivated by a desire for their lives to matter, to be validated by an accomplishment or purpose that is valued by those around them, and to build something that will survive even after they have left this earth.

Almost from the beginning of history men have strived to build and create that which is bigger, better, more grandiose, and more epic than anything that had been experienced before. Something that would serve as a monument to their greatness. Think of the Great Pyramid of Egypt, the Great Wall of China, the Taj Mahal, the Empire State Building, the Hoover Dam, or the Golden Gate Bridge.

Each is a testimony to the ingenuity and ability of people responsible for them, a legacy of sorts that has survived their own individual stories.

Think about the nations who spent vast fortunes and many years in an effort to go faster and further than anyone has before. Many Americans can still recall when John Glenn made his historic orbit of the earth in a spacecraft in 1962. Just seven years later two men would travel to and walk on the moon, and by the mid-1980s America was roaring into the great unknown on the historic space shuttle. Individuals like Neil Armstrong, "Buzz" Aldrin, and Sally Ride—along with a few who sacrificed their lives in space—have been immortalized for their contributions to this monumental endeavor.

Or in business and industry, Henry Ford, John D. Rockefeller, Andrew Carnegie, and Cornelius Vanderbilt leap to everyone's mind as the men who started with nothing yet built vast empires and accumulated incredible wealth and power, all in their own personal quest for greatness. In recent years entrepreneurs and business magnates like Steve Jobs, Bill Gates, and Oprah Winfrey have taken center stage, joined by a host of individuals who have made their mark in music, movies, media, and entertainment.

You get where I'm going with all of this: whether we achieve it or not, we all want to make our mark on this world. Whatever our economic, educational, or social station in life, all people are wired for greatness. That includes you and me.

I believe those seeds of greatness are planted in the human heart by God Almighty, whose plan is for every person to grow in true greatness and destiny as it is defined in His eternal economy. That means living a life marked by favor with God and man, enjoying incredible blessing and prosperity, and enjoying immeasurable value toward God and others.

That is the destiny I am believing and declaring for you, and the reason I penned this book.

SEEDS OF GREATNESS ARE PLANTED IN THE HUMAN HEART
BY GOD ALMIGHTY, WHOSE PLAN IS FOR EVERY PERSON
TO GROW IN TRUE GREATNESS AND DESTINY.

THE WRONG PATH

The world's formula for greatness—selfishly pursuing wealth, material possessions, accomplishments, acclaim, and power—is the only path that most people are aware of. They think it is the model they must follow, so they do, to their own ultimate heartache. One of God's greatest sorrows is to watch multitudes following the wrong path to greatness, when true greatness—body, soul, and spirit—is right within their grasp if they would but follow His plan!

Just take a look around you and you can see individuals dedicating their entire lives to pursuits that can never bring them true satisfaction. I never cease to be amazed at the efforts people go through to find success on the football gridiron, basketball court, baseball diamond, soccer field, or other athletic arena. Beginning even as kids, some folks spend many years of time, tears, and sweat equity in a desperate effort to win a few moments in the limelight of athletic greatness. And yet, even if they are able to scratch and claw their way to the top, those moments are over all too quickly, usually stolen away by someone who is a little bit better—a little "greater," as it were.

Most people, in fact, despite the years they have dreamed and trained and competed, never quite make it to the top. Oh, they're good, maybe even superior in ability to many others. But in their minds, they never rose to the level of "great." I once heard that hundreds of young men are signed every year to a professional baseball contract, but only about 3 percent will ever play an inning for a major league team. For the other 97 percent, their personal quest for greatness will fall short.

How many skilled and successful athletes can we name throughout the years who, although undeniably at the top of their game, never won a Super Bowl trophy, a World Series ring, an NBA title, or other championship that defined greatness in their sport? There is a clear sense of disappointment that hangs over them, a lack of validation for all their accomplishments, a nagging sense that in the long run they fell short of the "greatness" they pursued for so long.

It's not just on the athletic field that people strive for illusive greatness, however. The enormous efforts people go through to be at the top in business, politics, media, music, and entertainment—all are tied in one way or another to a deep need to reach a high level of prestige and esteem and to be "somebody" in the eyes of the world. Maybe it is one more successful business deal or acquisition, another hit record, another trophy or award from their peers assuring them that they have reached the pinnacle of success.

The huge irony, of course, is that for those who *do* reach the plateau they have been assured will mark them as "great," the achievement is almost invariably hollow and anticlimactic. How often have we heard individuals testify to this truth? How about the football star who finally wins a Super Bowl and relishes the experience for the few moments of fleeting joy, but the glory of the moment is soon gone and he asks, "Is that all there is? Was it really worth it?"

Or take the successful business mogul who finds himself increasingly dissatisfied with every million he makes, realizing that no matter how much he accumulates in wealth, influence, and power, he somehow never finds happiness.

How many actors or entertainers reach the end of their lives—or their popularity with the public—only to find that they have been forgotten or that the accolades they receive now fail to satisfy?

King Solomon, considered one of the wisest men who ever lived, had immense wealth, was successful in many things, and tried everything under the sun, yet at the end of it all he put it this way: *"Meaningless! Meaningless!... Utterly meaningless! Everything is meaningless."*[2]

And yet our culture keeps trying, trying, trying, believing the lie that the world's greatness brings happiness!

DO YOU HAVE THE STUFF OF GREATNESS?

Now don't get me wrong! There is certainly nothing wrong with being a successful athlete, businessman, actor, singer, or entertainer, or in pursuing excellence in almost any endeavor on earth.

There are many fine people throughout history who have made their marks in this world because of their skills and success. But what about those who have tried and failed, or those whose lives, by all human accounting, are devoid of anything that could be counted as great in the eyes of others? Have they somehow missed out on achieving the ultimate prize of life—true greatness?

Or how about those who were blessed with great talent or skill in some particular area, but laziness, bad habits, an addiction, or some other self-imposed limitation held them back from reaching their true God-given potential? For example, while the legendary Mickey Mantle was considered one of the greatest baseball players of all time, in his later years he admitted that he was held back from all he might have accomplished by years of alcohol abuse—much of it during his playing days—that chipped away at his incredible skills and ultimately cut short his hall-of-fame career. "God gave me a great body to play with, and I didn't take care of it," Mantle revealed years after his playing days were over. "And I blame a lot of it on alcohol."[3]

Tell me, friend, are such people disqualified because of their choices and wrong turns in life? Has true greatness eluded them?

---

2. Ecclesiastes 1:2 NIV.
3. Mickey Mantle, "Time in a Bottle," *Sports Illustrated*, April 18, 1994.

How about your own experience? What dream do you hold deep in your heart? What do you want to accomplish or become that would bring you great satisfaction and joy to fulfill—something that would place a big exclamation point over your life? Is it finishing college and diving into a successful career? Is it building a thriving and prosperous business? Maybe you envision yourself as a gifted entrepreneur with a special ability to see a need and know how to make it profitable. Or have you always dreamed of becoming a skilled and successful musician, athlete, or someone else in the public eye? Maybe your dream of greatness means answering God's call as a pastor, teacher, or in some other aspect of ministry.

Now let me ask you: How would you feel if you were able to achieve your dream to the fullest? Just picture it: You've graduated summa cum laude and are immediately swept into your dream career, where you wow everyone with your aptitude for success in every venture. Or as an entrepreneur you have the "Midas Touch" that causes every project you're involved in to turn to pure gold. Or in the entertainment world your unusual talent is recognized, you shoot to the top, and you are recognized the world over. Or how about as that star athlete? There you are: the MVP your rookie year, and your team goes on to decisively win the championship.

Tell me: after all is said and done and you succeeded to the uttermost, would the greatness you achieved give you the happiness and joy that makes life worthwhile?

Or maybe you're at the other end of the spectrum, and through circumstances beyond your control, or through poor choices you have made in life, any success at all—let alone fulfilling a lifelong dream of personal greatness—seems as far away as the stars. Instead of dreaming, you're despairing. "The only thing I've been great at, Henry, is failure," you might tell me. "I don't think there is any way the dreams that I once had for life will ever be fulfilled. I've just gone too far down the wrong road."

GOD'S BLUEPRINT FOR YOU

Friend, whatever your circumstances in life, whether you're dreaming of success or your life and future seem hopeless, I have some good news for you. You have a champion in your corner who is committed to raising you up to greatness in every area of your life. In medieval times, a skilled and courageous knight would often step forward to champion the cause of someone weaker and in deep need—someone who would otherwise be overwhelmed and destroyed by the foe. In your situation, no matter what it is, God is your Champion, your Deliverer, your Advocate, whose presence in your life ensures your victory and success against the storms and any enemy who tries to destroy you. God created you for success and prosperity, and it brings Him great joy to position you for His greatness, to take you right where you're at, and lead you on a pathway of divine destiny. His Word is clear that those have been His thoughts from the time He created you. He tells us that He has a plan for each of us to prosper us and to give us a clear future and a bright hope.[4] Yes, God has greatness written boldly on the very blueprint of your life.

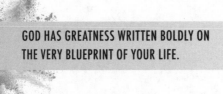

GOD HAS GREATNESS WRITTEN BOLDLY ON THE VERY BLUEPRINT OF YOUR LIFE.

But let me be crystal clear: the greatness I'm talking about does not begin or end with earthly success. True greatness for you begins in the very heart of God, where your value and worth never change. It is always solid gold. You see, in His eyes, every person is of equal value.

---

4. See Jeremiah 29:11.

27

No one has greater worth than anyone else. No one gets extra points by what he or she accomplishes, and no one is penalized for failure or weakness.

And so, when you come to Him, whether you are "the greatest" in the world's eyes, with a massive bank account and all that success can give, or you consider yourself a miserable "failure" because of difficult circumstances, your own mistakes, or even because of the actions and attitudes of others, the opportunities before the heavenly Father are equal: you are entitled to come to His throne of grace, mercy, and abundance with boldness and the expectation that He will hear and answer all your petitions.

It is important to remember that none of us come to God by our own righteousness and good works. In fact, the Bible emphasizes that every person on earth comes to God empty-handed, sinful, and in deep need of a Savior—and the only One who meets the requirements to be that Savior is God's one and only Son, Jesus Christ.

NOT BY YOUR GOODNESS

Now, I know it is not popular in this day and age to talk about sin. It's much easier—and more politically correct—to talk about misfortune, mistakes, and weaknesses. But please hear me: in order to reach the destiny of success and greatness to which God has called you in every area of life, you must start with the realization that sin— your actions, attitudes, and heart condition that run counter to God's Word—prevents you from being God's child and enjoying all the benefits of being a part of His family.

The good news is that when Jesus came to earth, died a cruel death, rose again, and went back to heaven to sit down at the right hand of the Father, He did it for one reason: to destroy the power that sin, sickness, death, poverty, and failure had over you, and to make you an absolute, no-holds-barred child of God with all the rights and blessings that come with that designation.

When you take responsibility for your sin and all its consequences of failure and defeat, admitting to the Lord that you are not able to chart your own course, it is at that moment that the true seeds of greatness begin to germinate in your life. A great exchange takes place, as God removes the rags of your past failures and misery, replacing them with a robe of greatness and authority.

The Bible tells us that because God's children are made new through Jesus Christ, we actually take a seat in the spirit next to Him in *"heavenly places,"* where we have great power and authority to reign and rule wherever He has planted us.[5]

Now you might say, "Henry, you don't understand. I've blown it so many times. I've failed in everything I've tried. My past sins and mistakes are just too heavy." Friend, I've had hundreds of conversations with people who have told me these very things, or who have complained that they just haven't been given the breaks others have enjoyed, or who insist that they've been cursed with "bad luck" or have just had too many "bad breaks."

I tell those people the same thing that I am telling you right now: your life as a child of God isn't based on your failures, on "luck," or on having the right breaks. If you will simply choose it, your life can be totally guided by God's favor. God tells you that as His child, you have the true seeds of greatness—of His authority and power—deep inside you, and that because He is for you, *nothing can stand in your way.*

The same God who gave us His own Son to purchase you back from the realm of misery and destruction is the one who promises to freely open His storehouse to ensure that you have everything you need to be truly great, successful, and excellent on this earth—in whatever realm He has called you.

---

5. Ephesians 2:6.

YOU ARE JUST LIKE ABRAHAM!

The Bible says that as God's child through Jesus Christ, you are an heir of Abraham, one of the greatest men of the Bible. You are subject to the same promises God gave to Abraham! Let me tell you, friend, that that means you have the same seeds of greatness inside you, controlling your destiny.

When God called Abraham out and up into his destiny, He promised to make Abraham into a great nation, to bless him and his descendants with abundant increase, to make his name famous and distinguished, and to cause him and his seed to be a blessing to others wherever they went.[6]

But when God made that promise, there was a major obstacle in the way. Abraham had no son, and his wife, Sarah, was barren— unable to have children. In other words, there was no way other than God's direct intervention that the greatness He promised was going to come to pass in Abraham's life. Only by believing God's promises, following God's plan, and staying in faith, would Abraham be able to experience what God had promised him.

The same thing is true for you. The greatness God has promised you, placing it deep within your heart, will only come to fruition as you look to Him, obey His word, and keep your heart and mind encouraged and positive. That is what faith in God is all about. The Bible defines it as an assurance and confidence of what we are hoping for, and the absolute conviction that it is a done deal even before it happens.[7]

Even though Abraham is considered one of the Bible's major -league champions of faith, we know that, just like you and me, he too had to battle against doubt and fear. In fact, Scripture tells us of a disastrous choice he made when he took his eyes off of God as His provider and began to rely on human reason.

---

6. See Genesis 12:2.
7. See Hebrews 11:1.

You see, God had promised that Abraham's heir would come through his wife Sarah. But after years of waiting and wondering, during which Sarah had no children, Abraham's faith began to falter, and he decided to "help" God by having a child with Sarah's handmaiden—an act of disobedience that changed the course of history.

However, that misstep in Abraham's walk of faith did not cause God to change His plan and promise in Abraham's life. No, God's mercy, grace, and favor was still in operation, and after leading Abraham through the wilderness and seasoning him in faith through years of perseverance, God capped it all off with an incredible miracle, causing Sarah to bear the promised heir, Isaac, when she was an old woman and well past child-bearing years.

YOU ARE NOT DISQUALIFIED

There is a lesson in Abraham's life for all of those who think that their past mistakes and failures have disqualified them from experiencing God's best for their lives. While it is true that there were serious consequences that came as a result of Abraham's doubt and disobedience, in the history of faith's champions written in Scripture, there is no mention of Abraham's misstep! What's recorded instead is a testimony of his commitment to believe God until the promise came to pass.

Likewise, in each of our lives, God looks past our failures, missteps, shortcomings, our fear, doubt, and unbelief, and He fixes His eyes on the divine destiny—that place of greatness—He has ordained for each of us. When we turn to Him in repentance and renew our commitment to believe Him and His Word, to follow His leadership, and to wait for His timing, God is emphatic and intentional in His response of favor on our lives. His love for us is so deep, His commitment to our success is so complete, that He will spare no expense from His unlimited storehouse and withhold no intervention from the angelic troops who await His orders, until His will is completed in the lives of His weakest and most needy children.

I am reminded of the story of British sprinter Derek Redmond, who was a favorite to win the 400-meter sprint at the 1992 Olympics in Barcelona. Derek posted the fastest time in the first heat, and went on to win his quarterfinal race. But in the semifinal, something disastrous happened. Half-way through the race, as Derek was near the front of the pack, his hamstring snapped and he fell to the ground terribly injured and in agonizing pain. As he lay there in agony of both body and emotions, he realized that not only were his hopes for an Olympic gold medal over, but quite possibly his whole competitive career as well. No one would have blamed him had he waited for a stretcher to carry him away to weep alone and in obscurity. But that's not what happened.

After a few seconds—but well after all other runners had crossed the finish line—Derek picked himself up, and while still in excruciating pain and anguish, began to hobble toward the finish line, determined to complete what he had begun. Before long, cheers began to go up throughout the crowd as spectators rooted for this man who would not quit, even in apparent defeat.

But that's not the end of this inspiring story. After a few a minutes, a much older gentleman could be seen fighting past Olympic security to get onto the track. This man ran straight for Derek and held him up as he struggled through tears and pain toward the finish line. That man was Jim Redmond, Derek's father, who had been with the young athlete right from the very beginning, guiding, encouraging, mentoring, and cheering his son on through long years of training. As the father witnessed the determination of his son to finish the race despite pain and deep disappointment, Jim whispered to Derek, "Let's finish this together." And so, as the world looked on and cheered, father and son hobbled toward the finish line, one filled with pain and disappointment, the other bursting with pride.

Friend, that is how it is with you and your heavenly Father. He has been with you right from the beginning, holding you up, encouraging you, mentoring you, carrying you through all your victories, disappointments, valleys and mountaintops, even during those times when you lost your way. He knows how hard you have tried, and the pain you have felt when you have fallen short, made mistakes, took wrong turns, and even given up for a time. Though it seems like you're not going to make it, that there is no reason to continue, He steps through the mist of your despair to say, "Let's finish this together."

God is not angry or upset with your failures and weaknesses. On the contrary, He is your greatest champion and advocate, constantly whispering to you in His still, small voice: "I am with you. I won't leave you. I will order your steps and make the path ahead of you straight and clear. Just keep your eyes on Me."

> JESUS HAS ALREADY WON THE VICTORY FOR YOU.
> ALL YOU HAVE TO DO IS STAND IN WHAT IS ALREADY YOURS.

GREATNESS IS WAITING FOR YOU!

No, God never said that the road ahead of you would be free of obstacles, trials, and testing. He never said you wouldn't be tempted, or that He would make sure you didn't fail. In fact, the opposite is true.

The Word of God tells us that the enemy of our destiny will challenge us over and over with many different attacks designed to derail us from the greatness God has intended for us. The good news, however, is that God has promised to take us successfully through every one of these assaults and give us victory even in the midst of trials.

The key is to remember that Jesus has already won the victory for us, and all we have to do is stand in what is already ours. Jesus made it clear that we would face trials, frustration, and even danger. But take courage, be confident, and don't be alarmed, He added, for "*I have overcome the world.*"[8]

Whatever you have gone through in your past, despite what you are facing today, and whatever tomorrow will bring your way, you can have the assurance that you are more than a conqueror! Your destiny is guaranteed because you are one of God's favorites. Right now, in spite of your past, your feelings, what others have told you about yourself, or the lies the enemy may have used to keep you from moving ahead, I want you to make three bold declarations and keep making them in the days and weeks ahead: "Father, I receive Your mercy and complete cleansing over all my past. Father, I embrace Your unchanging love for me. And right now, Father, I choose to walk into the destiny and greatness that You created me for even before I was born. In the name of Jesus."

Friend, God's greatness is waiting for you, and I can't wait to see it unfold!

---

8. John 16:33.

THE SEEDS OF TRUE GREATNESS
ARE ALREADY PLANTED INSIDE YOU!

FAVOR
TAKEAWAY

2

KEEPING YOUR FAITH FOCUS

As the president of a Christian university, I regularly have the opportunity to interact with men and women who are hard at work preparing for their futures. It's a joy to hear their hearts as they look with hope toward careers in a variety of business and professional fields and to dream with them about how God's plan for their lives will unfold.

However, as I speak with many of these young people, I often hear a note of concern about how to succeed in an increasingly uncertain world. With a job market that is getting more and more competitive, and with layoffs, outsourcing, and company closures filling newspaper headlines, I can fully understand their worry. "Will there be a place for me when I graduate, Bishop Fernandez?" they ask me. "What can I do to maximize my opportunities?"

My counsel to these individuals on the cusp of great life adventures is always the same, and what I tell them goes for everyone looking for their place in this world: Prepare diligently in every way possible to be the best you can be. But above all seek to maintain an uncompromising faith and trust in God for your future. I can tell you with absolute authority that faith in your heavenly Father—that is, a consistent confidence that He will guide your life and make your path straight—is the foundation for every success in life.

Scripture is clear that without faith it is impossible to please God. Jesus emphasized that with even just a little faith—only the size of a mustard seed—you can move mountains in your life and see doors open that would be locked tight in the natural. That one word— *faith*—comprises the simple formula for all the success you will need in life.

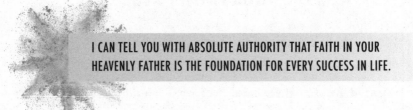

I CAN TELL YOU WITH ABSOLUTE AUTHORITY THAT FAITH IN YOUR HEAVENLY FATHER IS THE FOUNDATION FOR EVERY SUCCESS IN LIFE.

WHAT THE WORLD PREACHES

Be aware, however, that the world will give you a far different formula for success and achievement. The enemy of your soul has designed this formula specifically to cause you to compromise your faith and the eternal values that are crucial to God's destiny for you. While that compromise may begin subtly—a little fudging of the truth, a shortcut in your integrity, following worldly advice rather than bathing your plans in prayer—in the end it will overshadow your every decision. Think about it. For most of the world, actions like cheating, lying, stealing, and putting oneself ahead of others have become part of the formula of choice for "succeeding" in school, on the job, and in other areas.

While cheating in high school and college used to be considered grounds for failure and expulsion, many studies today reveal that it is actually expected behavior, from the poorest performers to the top of the class. In the workplace, dishonesty toward one's employer has practically become an entitlement, with even those considered top employees finding creative ways to punch in late or leave early, steal goods and services, and in general put themselves first to the detriment of those who sign their paychecks.

There was a time not so long ago when integrity was honored and valued, but today those who insist on it often face ridicule from a society that has grown jaded by rampant corruption in nearly every sphere.

Across our culture pilfering and theft have almost become second nature—even among some of God's own people. Tell me, have you ever stolen Internet service from a neighbor, logged in to someone else's online movie account, or downloaded a song or movie without paying for it? God calls this behavior stealing, and such compromise simply will not comport with a lifestyle of godly prosperity and success.

Or how about in the area of relationships and morality? While cheating on one's spouse used to be a shameful thing, our culture today increasingly celebrates and encourages unfaithfulness in many forms in the name of love.

The themes loud and clear in movies, TV, music, and online content are aggressively pushing people to take what they want from whom they want, with no regard for the consequences to oneself or others. And the statistics for broken homes and marriages—even among professing Christians—are astounding. Today, one out of three marriages ends in divorce—and many aren't even bothering to get married at all.

EVERY PERSON'S BATTLE

Friend, the truth is that every person has to face the temptation to compromise in some area of life. Maybe for you that doesn't mean lying, cheating, or something similarly obvious. Instead, perhaps you've found yourself relying too much on your own efforts, abilities, and "street smarts" to succeed, rather than surrendering your ways to God. If you were honest with yourself, you would have to admit that you have made decisions and choices in life that you knew were not pleasing to God and that were a compromise of your faith in Him and of the destiny He intended for you. You, as well as the rest of us, have trusted in education, a job or career, a relationship, or other efforts of your own, instead of putting God and His priorities first in your life.

Maybe it has meant opening a door in life that should have remained closed, or making a choice when you actually heard God's still, small voice encouraging you to make the opposite choice. Or maybe it was a decision that you knew would be detrimental or destructive to another person, just because it suited your needs or desires at the moment.

If any of the above describes you, you are not alone. For too many of us, trusting God has become little more than an empty confession rather than a vital relationship. We say the right words and go through all the motions, but in reality, as Jesus said, our hearts are far from Him.[1] We have placed ourselves at the head of our lives, and we have many idols that rank higher than our heavenly Father.

If, like Job, we were to begin to slowly lose the things we treasure—careers, bank accounts, homes, cars, belongings, or maybe even health and family—would the spiritual results be catastrophic? Like the foolish man Jesus spoke about who built his house on sand, too many individuals have built on the wrong foundation, and when the winds of adversity blow against their world, the destruction of all they have will be great. Many of them will even be offended at God because what they thought was *faith* was nothing more than *words*.

But friend, it doesn't have to be that way for you. God has made it clear that it is His good pleasure to give you the things that make for a successful life in His economy. His only requirement for such a blessing is a heart that is above compromise. A heart that is focused

---

1. See Matthew 15:8.

on loving and trusting Him. Jesus tells us that the key to living in the center of God's perfect will is to seek His kingdom and righteousness above everything else, and *"all these things"*—that is, everything that we have need of—will be given to us.[2]

You see, the heavenly Father knows the things we need before we even ask Him, and just like a good father, He will make sure that His blessings overtake us.

> JESUS TELLS US THAT THE KEY TO LIVING IN THE CENTER OF GOD'S PERFECT WILL IS TO SEEK HIS KINGDOM AND RIGHTEOUSNESS ABOVE EVERYTHING ELSE.

NO COMPROMISE

One of the secrets of walking in faith without compromise is intentionality—that is, making the determination moment by moment to pursue a lifestyle of faith and righteousness. You see, such a life doesn't happen by accident.

Take the example of Daniel, the Old Testament prophet, who along with his three friends, Shadrach, Meshach, and Abednego, was part of a group of handsome, smart, top-notch young Jewish men brought into the kingdom of Nebuchadnezzar to be educated and raised up in the Babylonian system. Now, as you read his account found in the book of Daniel, it is clear that these were upright young men, committed to following God regardless of the personal cost. They were men of integrity and without compromise.

The problem was that they had been thrust into a situation in which God was not honored and an upright, righteous lifestyle was

2. Matthew 6:33.

no value to their superiors. Ultimately these men of God would face some very tough choices—life-and-death ones—that challenged their commitment to integrity, righteousness, and faith. The choices these men made would determine their futures and their very lives.

In one of the earliest tests Daniel and his friends, along with the others in their group, were fed the rich, royal, and indulgent food and wine from Nebuchadnezzar's own table, as they went through a three-year process of training and education in the service of the king. Apparently nothing was considered too good for this group of fine young men, and they were to have plenty of it.

But something deep within the hearts of Daniel, Shadrach, Meshach, and Abednego revolted at the thought of being exposed to the unrestrained and indulgent lifestyle that was prevalent in the king's household. They knew that their lives were set apart, that they had been called to a higher place and purpose, and that regardless of the path the others followed, they were constrained by God to a higher standard. After a lot of prayer Daniel and his friends determined that they would not allow themselves to be compromised by enjoying what they knew in their hearts was not right.

Now I'm sure the other guys in training with them had a few choice words for the "holier than thou" attitude of these no-compromise men of God. "Come on, Daniel," they probably said. "Live it up! The king wants us to have these things. In fact, he's *ordered* us to follow this lifestyle. What's it going to hurt to enjoy the good things of life? You know you want to. You need to get on the same page as everyone else. Don't make waves."

In your own efforts to follow God, walk in faith, and see His best unfold in your life, you are also going to face invitations to compromise. But if you, like Daniel and his friends, determine beforehand that under God's authority you will stand strong, I guarantee you will make it—and it will be worth the sacrifice.

Daniel had to convince his Babylonian superior that the course of action he and the other three had determined to take was the right one. "It will be my head if you don't measure up to the king's standards!" this Babylonian, motivated by fear, told Daniel. But Daniel, knowing that following God's plan will always lead to success, challenged the official to put God's way to the test. "Allow me, along with my three close friends Shadrach, Meshach, and Abednego, to eat just vegetables and drink only water, and at the end of ten days compare our condition with that of the other men who continue to indulge in all that the king's table has to offer," he said.[3]

Of course, at the end of those ten days, Daniel and his three friends were healthier, stronger, more alert, and in better condition in every way than the other men. Moreover, because these men of God purposed to keep themselves in faith and close relationship with God, regardless of the personal sacrifice, God blessed them above all the other participants in the program, so that at the end of three years of training there was no one like them in ability and understanding. In fact, these Jewish men, who were actually prisoners and exiles from their own country, outpaced even the Babylonian experts, and were given top positions in the kingdom. God honored their refusal, in faith, to compromise in any way.

YOU ARE CALLED TO A HIGHER PLACE

Just as in Daniel's day, God is still today searching for men and women who will not compromise in the face of what the world and its system demand. One Scripture says that His eyes search throughout the whole earth looking for those whose hearts are perfect—without compromise or division—in the pursuit of Him.[4]

Friend, those are the ones whom God takes great pleasure in blessing with favor, prosperity, and great influence. Are you one of those? If God's eyes rested upon you, what would He see? What are the things

---

3. See Daniel 1:11–13.
4. See 2 Chronicles 16:9.

you are pursuing in life? Is your main focus getting a good education, having a good job, and creating a career that is going places? Is your goal to get ahead, build your investment portfolio, and make absolutely sure that you are financially set for life?

Or is all you do and pursue in life motivated by loving God, following His leadership, and pleasing Him in every way?

Now be assured that God is not against your preparations for success, a fulfilling career, or provision for your family. In fact, prosperity in body, soul, and spirit is part of His plan for His people. According to God's Word, the most prosperous people on earth ought to be His people.[5] As I said at the beginning, the desires, goals, and dreams that lie deep in your heart to succeed and prosper were put there by Him, and nothing pleases Him more than when you succeed at whatever you put your hand to do. You were created for greatness in His kingdom. But at the end of the day it must all be for *His* glory—not yours!

When we come to the end of our lives and stand before the King of Kings and Lord of Lords, everything we have accomplished in life, every trophy we have accumulated, and every honor that has been bestowed upon us, if it has not been submitted to His Lordship, will be burned up by His brightness and destroyed by His matchless glory.

I often counsel people who have spent years of effort and toil pursuing the things that this world says are important—a better job, higher income, a bigger house, nicer clothes, more vacations, prestigious schools for their kids. Some have gotten the success they seek, others are partway there, and still others are trying to gain a foothold on their way to the top.

But there is one thing all of these people have in common. If knowing and loving God is not their first priority, for all of their clawing and pursuing and getting and spending, they have little joy and little sense of accomplishment. That is because the world's system is not

---

5. See 3 John 1:2.

built for joy and satisfaction. It is meant to keep people dissatisfied, unfulfilled, and constantly seeking for more.

The Bible calls it *"leanness into their soul."* When God was leading His people out of Egypt and into the Promised Land of abundance, it seemed that no matter how much He blessed them in the wilderness, they always ended up dissatisfied, grumbling, and wanting something else. God's blessings weren't good enough for them, so, the psalmist says, God let them have what they lusted after, but with it put *"leanness into their soul."*[6]

It is interesting that Daniel and His friends kept their hearts tuned in to God's heart while surviving on a lowly, simple diet of vegetables and water. But look at the result: they grew strong in both body and spirit, and God blessed them with great success. By contrast, their counterparts were given what the Babylonians—the world's system—had defined as the necessary diet for success, but while they were given everything they wanted, at the end of the day they were found woefully lacking.

MAN SHALL NOT LIVE BY BREAD ALONE

Yes, diet is crucial not just for your body, but for your spirit as well—the part of your being to which God most clearly communicates. Jesus said that only God's Word can feed and nourish our spirits. The things the world will offer you—things that the apostle John explains satisfy your fleshly desires and your pride—will ultimately bring nothing but destruction and death to your dreams and destiny.[7] You can't hold on to those things while trying to love God and follow His path for you. John said that the world's system and all it offers will ultimately pass away and leave you hopeless and helpless.

Think about it! In a physical sense, what you eat can either energize you or make you sluggish and dull. Like me you've probably

---

6. Psalm 106:15 KJV.
7. 1 John 2:16.

had those moments when you knew you should eat an apple or a nice crisp piece of celery to satisfy those mid-afternoon hunger pangs. But instead you find yourself enjoying a gooey pastry or super-sized candy bar. And what's the result? Twenty minutes later you're fighting the inevitable sluggish feeling that comes with gorging yourself on something that is not good for you.

In the same way, how many times have you satisfied the urge for diversion by surfing the Internet, watching a questionable movie, or flipping through a worthless magazine, when your spirit is crying out for God's Word, quiet time in His presence, a few minutes of worship music, or a good teaching CD? God is constantly calling us up to a higher place of authority, and it is up to us to make those moment-by-moment decisions that will move us in the direction we know we need to go.

I am sure there were days when Daniel got up and eyed the king's table with a sense of longing. Those other men probably baited Daniel and his three friends as they enjoyed the rich food, wine, and other luxuries while the Israelite men subsisted on water and vegetables. "Why Daniel, you're all skin and bones," I can hear them say. "You're on the wrong track." But all the while, deep inside, Daniel was building himself up in his faith, saying, "Lord, I know You will sustain me. There's more to life than this. You have never let me down. You promised me a destiny and great favor if I would persevere, and that is what I will do!"

Likewise, there are folks in your life who will question and criticize the choices you have made to live above compromise. Friends, family, coworkers, and others may be following a whole different track in life. They don't have the perspective of God's Word tempering their decisions and giving them direction. They may even appear to have it all together. They will call you a fool for refusing to follow them—for refusing to compromise the destiny God has for you.

The apostle Paul was addressing this issue when he explained that the *"natural man"*—that is, the man who is living his life focused on this world's system rather than faith—cannot know the things of God because they can only be understood in a *spiritual* dimension.[8] Man looks on the outward appearance of things, but God has an inward, eternal perspective—and it is just such a perspective that He is sharing with you, a perspective that will always lead you toward His perfect will for your life. Jesus said that His words are *"spirit, and they are life"*[9] and they will sustain you through every circumstance you face, and make you prosperous in whatever you set your hand to do.

And at the end of the day, those around you—those who questioned and criticized your determination not to compromise your faith in God—will have to admit that, compared to those who follow the systems of the darkness of this world, you look much fairer, brighter, more peaceful, and more prosperous in body, soul, and spirit. What is more, whatever life throws at you, you will be able to handle with faith and a calm assurance that God is in control and will bring you to your desired destination.

Friend, in this day and age when great throngs of people are following the worldly path to success and prosperity, God is raising up a remnant of people who will stand up in this culture and say: "As for me and my house we will serve the Lord. We are going to feed on God's Word, fill our hearts and minds with the things that will reinforce faith, and we are going to reject the world's system. We will prosper under God's standard."[10]

YOU WILL PAY A PRICE

But be aware that even in the midst of your prosperity and blessing, you will pay a price for your no-compromise, God-focused approach to life. While the world may acknowledge your success, and even publicly praise you, more likely than not it will hate you for it and the enemy will use those around you to try to destroy you for your

---

8. 1 Corinthians 2:14.
9. John 6:63.
10. See Joshua 24:15.

stand. Let's take another look at Daniel's friends, Shadrach, Meshach, and Abednego. While their lifestyle of faith and righteousness before God opened the door to prosperity and advancement, there were evil men lurking in the shadows waiting for an opportunity to see them fail.

King Nebuchadnezzar set up a high golden image in Babylon and demanded all his subjects to bow down and worship it. He was understandably angry when a group of Babylonian busybodies informed him that Shadrach, Meshach, and Abednego had refused. Immediately the king summoned them and gave them an ultimatum. "You're no better than anyone else in my kingdom," I can hear him say to these godly men. "But you seem like nice guys. So I'm going to give you one more chance. Bow down and worship my idol—or burn in a fiery furnace I've prepared just for troublemakers like you."[11]

I love the response these humble servants of the Lord came back with to this arrogant, self-absorbed king. "*O Nebuchadnezzar, we have no need to answer you in this matter,*" they replied. "*If that is the case, our God whom we serve is able to deliver us from the burning fiery furnace, and He will deliver us from your hand, O king. But if not, let it be known to you, O king, that we do not serve your gods, nor will we worship the gold image which you have set up.*"[12]

What an awesome declaration of faith in God, given at a time when things couldn't have looked more hopeless in the natural for these men. Friend, think about your own circumstance. Have you prepared your heart to be faithful and steadfast in times of great stress? Ask yourself: how would you respond to demands that you compromise the faith that took Jesus all He had to win for you? What if your employer demanded that you do something underhanded or dishonest—something that no one would ever be able to expose? Would you have the courage, the Holy Spirit fire, to humbly, but boldly, decline?

---

11. See Daniel 3.
12. Daniel 3:16–18.

What if you were someday required to deny your faith in God in order to keep your job, have a place to live, or buy food for your family? What if, like these men, your life depended upon whether or not you denied Jesus? You may think that these are unlikely scenarios, but I believe that, just as is happening now in some parts of the world today, men and women right in our own communities and neighborhoods are going to face these kinds of choices, maybe even to the point of life or death.

These three men knew full well that unless God delivered them they were going to perish, and it is obvious that long before that day arrived, they had settled in their hearts where they stood. When those Babylonian soldiers threw Shadrach, Meshach, and Abednego into the fiery furnace that Nebuchadnezzar had heated up seven times hotter than normal in his arrogant rage, these men didn't go cringing in fear. Instead, they walked confidently into the fire with a calm assurance that, live or die, they were in God's perfect will and under His hand of protection.

That, of course, is where God desires each of us to live every day of our lives. Jesus made it clear that we will face hardships, turmoil, and tribulation that will try our faith—sometimes to an intense degree. But in the midst of such hardships God said we could have a peace that literally goes beyond our understanding. And why is that? Because, He assures us, *"I have overcome the world."*[13]

Friend, I am here to assure you that you can be an overcomer in every area of life. Whatever fiery and intense trial you face in your quest to go all the way in God's destiny for you, you can do so knowing that—whatever the outcome—God has your life in His hands, and He will go with you through the fire and bring you out victorious.

When Shadrach, Meshach, and Abednego were cast into the furnace, the heat was so intense that it killed the soldiers throwing them in. But as King Nebuchadnezzar gazed into the furnace, he was

13. John 16:33.

astonished to see, not three, but *four* men, walking unharmed in the midst of the flames. And the fourth man was like the *"Son of God"*![14]

Whether this fourth man was, indeed, the Son of God, or an angel sent from God's throne room to guard and protect His choice servants, those men stepped out of the fire whole and unharmed—and I believe the praises of God were on their lips for the great and mighty deliverance they had just experienced.

COUNT THE COST

There is an old saying that goes, "You've got to count the cost when you carry the cross." How true that is. While the gift of salvation through Jesus Christ is absolutely free, fulfilling the destiny to which God has called you will cost you something. In fact, it will cost you everything you have and everything you are. Jesus said that whoever would follow after Him would have to deny himself or herself, and *"take up his cross,"* with all that means.[15] That is the pathway to true success and greatness in every sphere of life. The cross of Christ represents the death of all of our worldly ambitions, selfish desires, and unsanctified goals. The apostle Paul put it this way: *"I am crucified with Christ: nevertheless I live...."*[16]

You see, when you surrender everything to Christ, when you "let go and let God" as someone once put it, you open the door to truly being alive and positioning yourself for God's richest blessings in your life. Gone are your own weak efforts, your compromise to a corrupt world's system, and your fear that you are going to miss out on something good.

Because you have settled in your heart and mind that God is in control of your destiny and no longer have to keep a tight hold on the reins of life, two awesome things happen.

---

14. Daniel 3:25.
15. Luke 9:23.
16. Galatians 2:20 KJV.

First, a calm assurance replaces the stress and worries that used to drive you, because you are no longer trying to accomplish what God promised He would do. I know from personal experience that allowing God to be God, instead of doing your own really bad imitation of Him and ending up falling flat on your face, is one of the most refreshing experiences in life. Knowing, and continuously acknowledging, that He is in control will do more to keep you in an attitude of overcoming victory than anything else.

Second, in your act of surrender to absolute faith in Christ and dependence upon Him, you actually give God access to work in your life in ways that may have been blocked before. You see, God is not going to pry your hands off the controls. You have to grant Him permission to take over. And when you do, amazing things can happen in your life and circumstances—things like financial prosperity, open doors of destiny, physical healings, and miraculous interventions that turn things around for you.

HOW GOD SEES YOU

I want to let you in on a little secret about how God sees you when you make the choice to follow Him without compromise—regardless of how many times you might think you're blowing it or missing the mark. The truth is that God sees and will respond to you in the same way He responded to Daniel, Shadrach, Meshach, and Abednego in their circumstances. They are a representation of God at work in your life. I am sure that these men of God struggled in the same way you and I do in our quest for God's best, and I am sure there were a few times when they missed the mark. But deep down they knew the secret of God's mercy and help, and as they regularly re-focused their commitment to living a life of faith without compromise, God was there to meet them when trials and hardships happened. He was faithful to place them in situations of influence and prosperity that were in keeping with the level of their faith walk.

Likewise, friend, as you continually commit to walking in the measure of faith that God has given you, He will bless you with advancement and prosperity in your realm of influence. You don't have to strive for it or work to be worthy of His blessings. All you have to do is receive them and continue to be faithful at the level to which He has called you.

It's a no-lose situation for you!

KEEPING YOUR FAITH FOCUS
MIGHT NOT BE EASY, BUT THE RESULT WILL BE
A LIFE BEYOND YOUR WILDEST IMAGINATION.

FAVOR
TAKEAWAY

3

YOU ARE CALLED AND CHOSEN

Have you ever watched a group of kids out on the playground choosing up sides for baseball or kickball? First to be picked, of course, are the natural athletes, the ones who can hit the ball out of the neighborhood or kick it halfway across town. Next come the ones who are good enough to hold their own in a game, followed by those who, at least, don't embarrass themselves or make mistakes that hurt their team's chances. Finally, the only ones left are the kids no one seems to want, those who have no skills and whose clumsiness causes the others to roll their eyes. There they stand by themselves in awkward, rejected silence after everyone else has been selected, waiting while the captains argue about who will be stuck with them. Or do you remember lunchtime at school? Remember the kids no one wanted to sit with because they were dirty and didn't dress nice, didn't smell the best, or had some handicap that made others feel uncomfortable?

In our everyday lives there are similar people with whom we come into contact, "fringe" individuals whom few seem willing to acknowledge, let alone befriend or embrace as valued and wanted. The homeless, the physically marred or challenged, the person with some trait or tendency that keeps him or her from fitting in.

On the job, in your neighborhood, even in your church or among your circle of acquaintances, there are such individuals, those who stand out from the talented, the popular, or even the average and ordinary. The ones whom few associate with. The marginalized.

It may be the man or woman with a tarnished reputation because of a criminal past or an immoral behavior or activity. It could be someone who is living a lifestyle that is condemned by society—or even by your church. Maybe it is a person whose birth or some other factor marks him or her as an outcast. Maybe it's you.

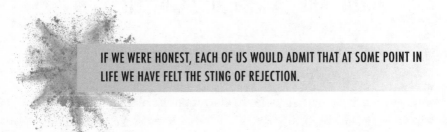

IF WE WERE HONEST, EACH OF US WOULD ADMIT THAT AT SOME POINT IN LIFE WE HAVE FELT THE STING OF REJECTION.

WE'VE ALL BEEN THERE

I think if we were honest, each of us would admit that at some point in life we have felt the sting of rejection. Nearly everyone at some time has been fired from a job, been sidestepped from a promotion or advancement, or lost out to someone else in an honor or award that they deeply wanted. We've all been in groups of people where it just seemed that we were not really wanted.

Some of us, of course, have suffered far deeper wounds through abandonment as children, unfaithfulness or divorce by a spouse, or some other devastating rejection at the hands of a person we loved or trusted.

For others, the feelings of rejection are based on an internal sense of inferiority and isolation they have carried around their entire lives. Somehow they have been convinced that they are not as good as others, or that people in general do not like them. How many times have we heard a parent or other adult denigrate a child with words we know are wounding and destructive—insults and accusations that have the power to leave scars for life.

Maybe you yourself have been the victim of such words, and for years they have echoed in your mind, haunting your efforts and holding you back from unfettered success and victory. Or perhaps the rejection and isolation you feel from those around you is based on your absolute inability to succeed in an area you have longed to conquer, or to see a door opened that would make all the difference in the world to your future. Your powerlessness to effect the change you desire has made you feel as if you are a failure. The sense of defeat has led you to put up a wall of self-isolation. Or maybe a past that you would rather forget, or your own birth or background, has caused you to feel rejected and unaccepted by others.

Whatever the reason for the sense of inadequacy, failure, or rejection, these feelings can turn into hopelessness and despair if you let them. If he can, the enemy of your soul will use them to convince you that destiny and accomplishment have passed you by. *I'll never be chosen*, you might think. *I'll never have the opportunity to succeed. I don't have what it takes. I lack the abilities, and my chances have passed me by. God has forgotten about me and I am doomed to defeat.*

GOD CALLS THE WEAK

For those who find themselves struggling with such thoughts, I have some great news! God, the Maker of heaven and earth, has not forgotten you. He hasn't passed you by for someone more talented, well-liked, or popular. In fact, I can declare with all confidence that He has both called and chosen you for success, destiny, and prosperity in every area of life, and you can begin right now to reject the lie that you are condemned to failure. How do I know it? Let me walk you through the process.

One of the foundational truths that drives the kingdom of God is His commitment to the weak, the marginalized, the outcast—in fact, everyone who is rejected and unchosen by society. If you look throughout Scripture and history, you will find that the ones God has used the most mightily are those who had very little to offer in the natural or who blew the earlier opportunities they had been given.

> ONE OF THE FOUNDATIONAL TRUTHS THAT DRIVES THE KINGDOM OF GOD IS HIS COMMITMENT TO THE WEAK, THE MARGINALIZED, THE OUTCAST—IN FACT, EVERYONE WHO IS REJECTED AND UNCHOSEN BY SOCIETY.

God tells us that He empowers for success those who are the most weak—physically, mentally, emotionally, financially. To those who are at their lowest He gives abundant strength.[1] Friend, that includes you, no matter how low you feel you have sunk, and how far you think you have drifted from the possibility of success. Let's look at some examples of the weak who have become strong through God's power.

God's own people Israel, were suffering under terrible oppression and the bondage of slavery in Egypt when He called out to them, reminding them of the promise He had made to their forefather Abraham to make them into a great and mighty nation. Now, I don't know about you, but when I read the account of the children of Israel in the book of Exodus, I am not too impressed by what I witness. They were a poor, weak, passive, and totally uninspiring group of people, convinced of their own defeat and failure. It is quite certain that there would have been no way they could have pulled themselves out of the misery and oppression which they were suffering from.

---

1. See Isaiah 40:29.

In fact, one might even wonder why God chose them in the first place! In the natural world there were certainly some better options available, people groups that were strong, confident, and going places—the Egyptians, for example. This mighty nation was like today's star athlete, music mogul, or power CEO of a wildly successful company. The Egyptian people had it together and were the most upwardly mobile society on earth at the time. Other nations feared them, and they could do whatever they wanted.

But God, then and now, isn't impressed by the power, might, and abilities that human beings can muster. Instead, His heart is turned toward those into whom He can pour His own unlimited power. Yes, that means you! The weaker and more incapable you find yourself on your own, the more He is able to be strong on your behalf and make you fruitful in every venture.

God told His people Israel that He chose them not because they were more numerous or greater than the others who lived around them. In fact, just the opposite was true. They were the fewest and least. He chose them, He said, because of the covenant He had made with their forefathers, particularly Abraham, whom He promised to make great and influential throughout the earth. He called Israel to be a special "set apart" people for Himself, through which He would demonstrate to the whole world His mercy and love.

Now, put yourself in that same situation, because that is precisely what God is saying to you right now! "I didn't choose you because of your abilities, talents, wealth, or anything else you could—or could not—offer," I can hear Him telling you. "I chose you because of the covenant I promised through Jesus Christ, a covenant to save you, heal you, restore you to your original destiny, and to prosper you in everything you set your heart and hands to do!"

And who did God choose to deliver this special people of His out of the bondage of Egypt? Again, it wasn't your typical champion with a lot of power, strength, and confidence. Instead, He called the lowly Moses, a man who had destroyed his opportunity as the adopted son of Pharaoh's daughter through murder. On the run from the Egyptian authorities, Moses found himself on the backside of the desert for an extended wilderness time. And it was there, at possibly his weakest and lowliest state, that God called and empowered Moses to go before Pharaoh and effect the deliverance of His people.

What a phenomenal testament to God's faithfulness! It is the same faithfulness and commitment that He has focused on you. And it is for a purpose that extends far beyond you and your concerns. God is committed to your prosperity and success so that it serves as a testimony of His love, His commitment, and His purpose in the lives of anyone who turns their hearts fully to Him. You are called to be a model of God's faithfulness!

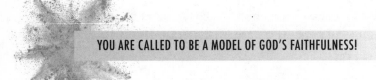

YOU ARE CALLED TO BE A MODEL OF GOD'S FAITHFULNESS!

HE SEES THE REAL YOU

Would you like to know another unlikely example of greatness through God's power? Let's take a look at David, the lowly Jewish shepherd boy who became a great warrior and king. When God sent the prophet Samuel to the home of Jesse to select a new leader for Israel, no one in David's family or surroundings—not even Samuel himself—thought that this fresh-faced boy had the stuff of which kings are made.

As one after another of Jesse's sons were brought before Samuel—masculine, strong, and impressive young men—the prophet said to himself, "Surely this fine-looking fellow is Israel's new king." But as each one passed by, God said no, this wasn't His choice, and He reminded Samuel that while humans are impressed with the outward appearance of a person, their beauty, stature, strength, talents, and renown, *"God looks on the heart."*[2]

That bit of news ought to give you great joy and hope, because despite any lack you might have in the way of talent, ability, natural strength, or anything else by which people typically measure success and potential—God sees your heart! Do you understand the implications of this revelation? Your only requirement for success and advancement in your divinely ordained destiny is having a heart that is right toward God. And the most important heart issue in God's eyes is humility—knowing your weakness and acknowledging your desperate need for His help.

> THE MOST IMPORTANT HEART ISSUE IN GOD'S EYES IS HUMILITY—KNOWING YOUR WEAKNESS AND ACKNOWLEDGING YOUR DESPERATE NEED FOR HIS HELP!

God knew He had a person He could choose and use in the lowly, humble shepherd boy everyone else overlooked. But He had to point David out to Samuel. "Do you have any other sons?" Samuel asked Jesse as the last of the obvious choices were finished. To which Jesse replied, "Well, yes, there is one more, but he is my youngest, David, and he is out tending sheep." Everyone involved in that scene was no doubt thinking, "Certainly David isn't God's choice for king! That will be obvious when Samuel gets one look at this kid."

Even Samuel must have felt doubtful as he commanded, "Send for the boy. We will not move on until we have taken a look at him."

---

2. 1 Samuel 16:7.

You probably know the story yourself. When the young boy stepped into the clearing and Samuel got one look at him, God made it clear that David was the one. "Arise and anoint him King of Israel, for he is My choice."[3]

What is it that made David worthy, when he had none of the qualities that Samuel or anyone else thought were needed in a king? While the 1 Samuel account doesn't specifically tell us, a look at David's life does.

Despite all the negatives in David's life, despite all the things that might have caused any one of us to reject David as unacceptable, God testified that David was a *"man after My own heart, who will do all My will."*[4]

So what does that mean in practical terms, and how can that apply to your life?

It's really very simple.

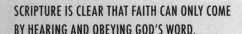

SCRIPTURE IS CLEAR THAT FAITH CAN ONLY COME BY HEARING AND OBEYING GOD'S WORD.

That "after-God's-heart" lifestyle means that David had an unswerving, uncompromising faith in God. Of course, that doesn't mean he never fell out of faith or made decisions and choices based on flesh or fear. But it does mean that the sum total of his life experiences exhibited a trust in God. From the time as a young shepherd boy when he slew a bear, a lion, and the giant Goliath, to his final days on earth when he passed on his authority to his son Solomon, David

3. See 1 Samuel 16:12.
4. Acts 13:22.

demonstrated a dependence upon his heavenly Father that is a perfect model for each of us.

HEART OF HUMILITY

And how did David develop such an historic and championship faith in God? It certainly didn't come naturally. It was because throughout his life David cultivated a deep love and undying devotion to God's Word. Scripture is clear that faith can only come by hearing and obeying God's Word.[5] And the apostle Paul explains that we go from doubt to faith by having our minds renewed by the Word of God.[6]

There is simply no more powerful resource for our success and destiny than God's Word. The more time you spend soaking up the truths of His Word, the more your thinking will line up with God's thinking.

That is what happened with David, and the reason he was so powerful and confident in faith. David writes in one place that unless God's Word had been his delight and focus, *"I would then have perished in my affliction."*[7] You see, David was not immune to trouble. Like you and me, he had his share of afflictions, heartache, rejection, and life concerns. But the secret to his overcoming faith was a devotion to God's Word. He built himself up constantly in the truths that would sustain him in times of crisis and need.

That process started before David faced hardships, so that when they came and he needed to trust God for help or an answer, he had a reservoir of truth stored up in his spirit. David said that hiding God's Word in His heart was what empowered him to overcome doubt, sin, and obstacles.[8]

---

5. See Romans 10:17.
6. See Romans 12:2.
7. Psalm 119:92.
8. See Psalm 119:11.

Now, one thing we know beyond a doubt is that David's later life was marred by some serious sin, including both adultery and murder. In our earthly estimation, God should have seen that coming and it certainly should have completely discounted David for God's blessing and use. But it didn't. But despite the fact that David exhibited a sinful side, despite the fact that he sometimes blew up in anger and responded irrationally, and despite the fact that, according to Scripture, he was less than stellar as a father to his children, David had one quality going for him that tipped the scales in his favor. It was that one quality that is so important to the heart of God: humility.

When David did slip up, when he sinned and needed to make things right, he was quick to bring his faults to the Lord. That is truly the heart of humility and central to seeing God's favor and direction in your life. God is clear that He will not turn away a person who is humble and contrite. He resists those who are proud, but pours out His mercy on those who are humble.[9]

Now that, of course, is not the way the world operates. Most people seem to think that in order to succeed you have to show some "attitude"—a little arrogance to make it clear to everyone that you are in control. But if you want to reach God's best for your life I encourage you to reject this kind of approach and go for godly humility. It will take you so much farther—all the way to the plans and purposes God has placed deep within your heart.

The secret to your success is a deep reverence for God and His ways. Those who are strong and wise in their own minds, those who are mighty or influential according to the world's standard, those who seek to be counted by the world as noble and esteemed—God passes all of these by in His search for the ones who will receive His richest blessings and rewards. His choice are those people who are, by the world's measure, weak, foolish, broken, worthless, and despised.[10]

9. See James 4:6.
10. See 1 Corinthians 1:26–29.

> **THE SECRET TO YOUR SUCCESS IS
> A DEEP REVERENCE FOR GOD AND HIS WAYS.**

MANY ARE CALLED, FEW ARE CHOSEN

Tell me, are you willing to count yourself as one of these "foolish" ones? Maybe your tendency is to be strong, self-confident, and assured. Your natural inclination would be to step away from being identified with weakness and need. If that is the case, let me encourage you to ask God to do a work in your heart so that you can count yourself worthy to stand with those whom God esteems. Jesus said that many are called to this walk of humility and complete dependence upon Him—but very few are actually chosen.[11] In other words, there aren't many who, in the long run, will allow themselves to become an instrument into which God will pour His Spirit without measure, and who will reap the rewards that He is willing to give.

But, friend, I have great confidence that you are both called and chosen. You are one of His elect, called to share in all that He has for humanity. Yes, God has called you to faith and humility so that you can be a full participant in His goodness: the complete healing, prosperity, and destiny that He planned for you from the very beginning.

In fact, the Bible declares that you are part of a chosen generation, a royal priesthood, and a holy, set apart nation. Central to your purpose in His kingdom is to show forth to this world the glory and praise of the mighty God who called you out of darkness and despair into *"His marvelous light."*[12]

---

11. See Matthew 22:14.
12. 1 Peter 2:9–10.

That is a powerful truth and promise that you ought to grab on to and never let go of. Make this a bold declaration over your past, present, and future! Knowing and living in this truth will make all the difference in reaching the destiny God has for you.

YOU ARE NEVER FORGOTTEN OR REJECTED;
YOU ARE CALLED AND CHOSEN.

FAVOR
TAKEAWAY

4

REJECTING FEAR, EMBRACING FAITH

In your lifetime journey of fulfilling God's destiny, you are faced with many choices. Some of the decisions you make have the power to impact you in many ways. Lifestyles and activities, both positive and negative, could lead you in a certain direction for years to come. For example, a choice to get involved in drug or alcohol use, or to enter into an unhealthy relationship, may lead to years of heartache and pain both for you and those you love. Conversely, committing to a lifestyle of prayer, the Word of God, and close fellowship with Jesus will undoubtedly place you on a course of rich fulfillment.

Some choices aren't necessarily right or wrong—God gives each of us grace and room to take different paths in life that will all lead to His blessing. Other important decisions may prompt you to a time of prayer as you seek God for His best. "Where should I go to college?" "Should I take this employment position that has been offered to me?" "Lord, is this the person you want me to spend the rest of my life with?"

> GOD GIVES EACH OF US GRACE AND ROOM TO TAKE DIFFERENT PATHS IN LIFE THAT WILL ALL LEAD TO HIS BLESSING.

THE MOST IMPORTANT CHOICE

There is one choice, however, that is more crucial and life-impacting than any other you'll make. In fact, your decision on this important issue will actually determine the quality of your choices in every other area of life. Grabbing on to this choice is foundational to your success in every area of life, from your career, to relationships, to prosperity and favor in your endeavors—and most importantly, how you advance in God's kingdom. I am referring to the choice you must make about whether you will live your life in fear or faith. The Word of God tells us that there is no greater a choice you can make in your life on a day-by-day basis than to have uncompromising faith in God.

You see, the enemy of your soul—and the enemy of your destiny—is in the fear business. That is his stock-in-trade. He doesn't actually have any true power over the life and destiny of the believer, because the blood of Christ has rendered him absolutely powerless. But that doesn't stop him from trying to influence Christians, using all of his satanic smoke and mirrors to try to convince those who ought to know better that their lives are out of God's care. His most effective tool is fear, and he uses it with incredible impact in the lives of many of God's people.

How many times have each one of us heard the voice of the enemy whisper to us things like:

You're going to lose your job.

You're not going to be able to pay your bills.

Your marriage is going to break up.

You're not going to be able to finish school.

You're going to lose your home.

You're never going to get well.

And that's just a handful of the more obvious lies the enemy uses to trip up God's people and plunge them into needless fear. The Bible describes Satan as a *"roaring lion"* on the prowl for whom he can attack and destroy. And there is only one way to defeat him. The Word of God commands us to *"resist"* the enemy by standing firm in our faith.[1]

There are only two alternatives. You are either going to live in faith or fall in fear and doubt. But friend, I have some great news for you. Jesus, the *"author and finisher"* of your faith,[2] has already paved the way for your victory. As you focus your attention on Him, you will be strengthened to face victoriously every attack the enemy throws at you.

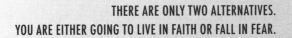

THERE ARE ONLY TWO ALTERNATIVES.
YOU ARE EITHER GOING TO LIVE IN FAITH OR FALL IN FEAR.

A CASE STUDY IN FEAR AND FAITH

Natalie is just such an example. The enemy pulled out all the stops in an attempt to drive her out of faith and into fear, to pull her away from her God-given destiny. From an early age Natalie's life was filled with hardship. Growing up in a home where turmoil ruled, as a young teen Natalie took to the streets where she thought she would find acceptance and the love she craved. Instead, her world quickly spiraled

1. 1 Peter 5:8–9.
2. Hebrews 12:2.

completely out of control in an atmosphere where drugs, immoral life-styles, and criminal behavior were the norm.

After years of such living, Natalie ultimately found herself a desperate single mom of two in search of some answers. One day at her job, a coworker shared the good news of Jesus with her, and Natalie embraced the salvation, deliverance, and new life that Christ offered.

Of course, following a few weeks of unspeakable joy that every believer experiences after surrendering control to the Savior, Natalie began to be confronted by the inevitable lies of the enemy, as he brought up all of the sin from which Christ had freed her. "Don't think people have forgotten your past life, and the terrible things you did," the enemy whispered. "You're never going to be free from those things. You made that bed and now you're going to have to lie in it for the rest of your life."

Natalie had plans of going to college and starting a career, but the enemy attacked her with lies designed to destroy her dreams and persuade her to give up. "No one in your family ever went to college," the enemy would taunt her. "You barely finished high school, and you don't have the ability to succeed. The road's too long and it's too much work."

But Natalie had been prepared by the pastor of her church to recognize those attacks for what they were: lies designed to fill her with fear and to doubt God's mercy and goodness. And she was surrounded by godly, mature individuals in her church body who stood with her, prayed for her, and encouraged her with the truth from God's Word.

And so, as the enemy hit her with the lie that her past would continue to haunt her, Natalie knew the truth: just as far as the east is from the west, God had removed her past and shame from her and replaced it with His righteousness.[3]

---

3. See Psalm 103:12.

When the enemy brought up past sins and shortcomings, Natalie countered with the truth that there was no condemnation in her life because she was firmly at rest in Christ Jesus.[4] And when she was attacked with fears that somehow she would be blocked from reaching the goals she had set as a child of God, Natalie declared the truth from His Word that God had spoken to her almost from the day that she gave her life to Him—that He had wonderful plans for her, laid out even before she was born, to prosper Natalie and her children, to fill their lives with peace where strife and turmoil had once reigned, to protect her and her family from the attacks of the enemy, and to ensure for her a future and a hope.[5]

WHAT DOES THE ENEMY TEMPT YOU TO FEAR?

Like Natalie, we all have a past that the enemy so effectively dredges up to taunt us. And we all have areas where the enemy tempts us to fear. From fear of failure, to fear of being haunted by our past, fear that we will lose our job or economic security, fear of sickness or death, or fear that we will lose someone we love—Satan seems to know the *exactly* right panic button to push in each of our lives that will threaten to move us from confidence and hope to fear and uncertainty.

God and His mercy are the only hope we have for safety and success in this life. In fact, *that* is the way God in His perfect wisdom planned the universe, so that our hope can be in nothing but Him. All the securities upon which we build our lives—health, career, money, relationships—all of that and so much more are as temporary as the wind. They may be gone tomorrow. But God has promised that He will never leave us nor forsake us, so that we can have the boldness to declare, "*The* LORD *is my helper, I will not fear.*"[6]

---

4. See Romans 8:1.
5. See Jeremiah 29:11.
6. Hebrews 13:5–6.

The Word of God defines faith as the confidence to receive that for which we hope and the assurance of the things we do not yet see.[7] God is asking each of us to put our trust in Him regardless of the circumstances in which we find ourselves and despite the fears with which the enemy confronts us. So if we are serious about increasing our faith and dependence upon God, for most of us it means that there are going to be some areas where we are going to be challenged.

Frankly, it is not that difficult to mouth words of faith when everything is going great and the skies are blue. But when hardships and difficulties come to our lives, many of us begin to realize how thin our faith really is, and how prone to fear we really are. In the life of the believer, these situations are opportunities to grow in faith, because, face it, most of us would never voluntarily step out into a larger place of believing God. We would rather play it safe. Going into areas of uncharted waters in our faith walk can be pretty scary, and it usually takes a little nudge from the Lord to take us to new heights in the destiny He has for us.

IT USUALLY TAKES A LITTLE NUDGE FROM THE LORD TO TAKE US TO NEW HEIGHTS IN THE DESTINY HE HAS FOR US.

GOD TESTS AND TEMPERS OUR FAITH

The Bible tells us that God puts each of us in situations that cause our faith to be tested and tempered so that we will learn how to persevere during times of trial.[8] One of the main secrets to reaching and

7. Hebrews 11:1.
8. See James 1:3.

enjoying the destiny God has for you is enduring until His promises come to pass in your life.

Take Tom, for example. He was a hard-working, self-determined individual who really loved the Lord and wanted to grow deeper in His faith. Throughout most of his life, Tom had pretty much paved his own way, relying on his abilities and efforts to get ahead. He made a good wage, faithfully paid his tithes and offerings, stayed current on his bills, and thanked God for blessing him. While Tom spoke sincerely about having a deep faith in God and His provision, it wasn't until he lost his job and things began to get tight that Tom's faith was really put to the test. When his company downsized and Tom found himself unemployed, he was forced to face how small his faith really was.

He realized he had been trusting in his job and in himself for security rather than in his loving heavenly Father.

Fear reared its ugly head as Tom began to worry about how he would make his house and car payments, how he would put food on the table for his family, and what the future would hold. In his desperation Tom had no other option but to throw himself and his family on God's mercy, crying out daily for God's provision. And as he did so, turning to God's Word for answers, Tom was struck by a simple—but profound—truth: God loves to provide for His children, and He wants us to have a sense of expectancy for that provision.

I love Jesus' words in the gospel of Matthew admonishing us to observe the birds of the air and the lilies that grow out in the wild. Neither of these creations of the heavenly Father worry about their daily needs, and yet God always provides the birds with plenty of food, and the lilies of the field are more gloriously arrayed than even King Solomon—one of the wealthiest and wisest men who ever lived.[9]

Friend, perhaps like Tom—and like so many other people in today's unstable world—you have found yourself living on the edge of

---

9. See Luke 12:24–28.

fear as you face an uncertain future. *Will I have a job tomorrow?* you might wonder. *How am I going to pay the bills and provide for my family? How am I going to get ahead? I thought God had an awesome destiny for me, but here I am wondering how I will make it through next week.*

Let me assure you that God has certainly not forgotten you, and because you are His valued child, He is not about to allow you to go without the things you need. However, as He does with all His children, He is going to test you and discipline you to drive out all the fear and bring you to a place of total dependence upon Him.[10]

When Jesus offered the illustration of the heavenly Father's caring provision for His creation, he wasn't addressing people who had no needs. He was speaking to individuals in first-century Israel who were genuinely concerned about their day-to-day existence. His counsel and promise to them is just as relevant today. "Don't worry about tomorrow!" Jesus said. "Instead, seek first and foremost to be in line with God's purposes, and all the things you need will be added to you."[11]

You see, if you will focus your love and attention on God, seeking to know Him better, to obey Him more fully, and to be found in a place of dependence upon Him, you will never be in want for anything. Your inheritance from God will be *"pressed down, shaken together, and running over."*[12]

GOD LOVES TO PROVIDE FOR HIS CHILDREN, AND HE WANTS US
TO HAVE A SENSE OF EXPECTANCY FOR THAT PROVISION.

---

10. See Hebrews 12:6.
11. See Matthew 6:33.
12. Luke 6:38.

THE IMPORTANCE OF CONFESSION

Of course, when you are in the midst of such testing and tempering by God, it is easy to begin wondering if He has forgotten about you. *Is God really going to come through for me?* you might ask yourself. *Does He see what I'm facing, the stress I am under, and how much I need a turnaround from His hand?* In those times it is important to embrace and confess God's promises. They have tremendous power to see you through!

Early in our marriage, God called my wife, Carol, and me to move to Florida, where years later He led us to start Faith Center Church in Fort Lauderdale and the University of Fort Lauderdale, which is raising up men and women to reach their destiny in Christ. But before He could accomplish those things through us, He first had to teach us how to stand in faith in the midst of situations that cried out for us to fear. He had to take us to "Faith School."

I remember one particular situation early on that taught me the goodness of God and how He *can* and *will* provide in the most difficult of circumstances. When Carol and I arrived in Florida, we faced one challenge after another, many of them dealing with finances because I didn't have a job and had no immediate prospects of obtaining one.

In the midst of this testing, I made a choice that I would begin to confess God's Word rather than question His goodness. On one particular day we were in desperate need of groceries, and I determined to put my faith on the line with God.

"Lord, You said that you would provide for all our needs, and so I am sticking to that promise," I said to Him in prayer that evening. "We don't have any money for groceries, and I know you didn't send us to Florida to starve. So I am believing You to provide for our needs just like you did for the children of Israel when You sent manna from heaven. I am not going to beg, borrow, or steal. I am going to wait in expectation with my eyes toward heaven."

Friend, God is not looking for perfect theology or repetition of a Scriptural formula. He looks at our hearts for a measure of faith, and when He sees it He will rush in with an answer that will blow us away with His goodness.

When I awoke the next morning—still with no money and no answer—I distinctly sensed God directing us to go shopping for groceries. So with an empty wallet and checkbook, Carol and I made our way somewhat sheepishly over to the local Winn-Dixie grocery store, where we began walking up and down the aisles, placing the items we needed in our grocery cart, with full expectation that at just the right moment God would provide the money we needed to pay for the groceries.

I have to admit that as we finished and made our way to the check-out line, with no money in hand, the palms of my hands were a little sweaty. What was I going to say to the check-out lady when she tallied up the total and held out her hand for payment? "Lord, I'm trusting in You, but I'm running out of time," I remember whispering to God under my breath. "Thank You for providing for our needs," I added somewhat timidly.

As I stood with Carol at the check-out lane, speaking to God in our need, out of the corner of my eye I saw a man from church step through the automatic doors of the grocery store, look around for a moment as if he were searching for someone, and then walk directly over to Carol and me. "Henry," he said, "I was at home this morning when God told me that you were over here at the Winn-Dixie and that you needed help buying your groceries."

And with that, as Carol and I stood and watched in amazement, this man who had heard God's voice and chose to obey pulled out his wallet and handed the money to the equally amazed check-out lady. That day we witnessed a valuable truth from God—a resounding truth that has been the foundation for all that God wanted to do in and through us: If we will stand in simple faith, refuse fear, and determine to confess God's Word in every circumstance, He will literally move heaven and earth to answer our prayers and meet every need.

> I WANT TO LET YOU IN ON A ONE OF THE MOST FREEING TRUTHS
> ABOUT THE KIND OF FAITH GOD IS SEEKING:
> IT DOESN'T TAKE A LOT AND IT DOES NOT HAVE TO BE PERFECT.

IT ONLY TAKES A LITTLE

Many folks are under the impression that God will only respond to perfect, giant-sized faith. But I want to let you in on one of the most freeing truths about the kind of faith God is seeking: it doesn't take a lot and it does not have to be perfect. Jesus said that if you have faith only the size of a mustard seed—so small it might seem insignificant—you can say to any mountain in your life, *"Be removed and be cast into the sea,"* and that mountain will have to obey. Do you get the picture of God's power at work in your life? A mustard seed of your faith versus a mighty, immovable mountain, and your faith will win every time![13]

The good news is that, while God wants your faith to increase and grow bigger as you exercise it, even frail, small, weak faith has incredible power to move mountains and obstacles out of your way. If you are honest with God about how weak and ineffective you feel, He will respond with His strength.

One time a man brought his demon-possessed son to Jesus' disciples, and when they could not get deliverance for the boy, the man turned to Jesus Himself. Jesus' instructions to the man were simple:

---

13. Mark 11:23.

"All things are possible to him who believes."[14] Grabbing on to that truth, the man responded with deep passion: *"Lord, I believe; help my unbelief!"*[15] And as everyone watched, Jesus responded to that man's small, weak, but fervent faith with a powerful healing for his son.

The same is true for you. Perhaps you feel absolute dread about the situations with which you are faced—a mountain of debt, a marriage that is dying, children who are lost in destructive lifestyles, an illness the doctor says is incurable, a future that appears bleak and hopeless.

Friend, God is not expecting a "faith performance" from you. And He is not looking for you to match what you see others doing. A lot of people shout the victory and speak a bold faith in public, but behind closed doors their words are filled with complaining, doubt, and fear. That is nothing more than double-mindedness, and God is clear that such people will not receive anything from Him.[16]

It is much better for you to be honest with yourself and God, confess the smallness of your faith, and ask God to help you have more of it. That is what I have done throughout my own life in Christ, and He has been so faithful to build up my faith through His Word, through the encouragement of friends and fellow believers, and through the experiences He has allowed me to face.

THE GOOD NEWS IS THAT, WHILE GOD WANTS YOUR FAITH TO INCREASE, EVEN FRAIL, SMALL, WEAK FAITH HAS INCREDIBLE POWER.

---

14. Mark 9:23.
15. Mark 9:24.
16. See James 1:6–8.

PERSISTENCE AND PATIENCE

Now remember that God's process of increasing your faith will not always be comfortable, just as getting in shape physically is not always comfortable. Increasing your endurance or building muscle mass only comes through a rigorous schedule of working out, lifting weights, running, doing aerobics, and other exercises. But if you persevere in the process, before long you find yourself making progress. You're losing the weight that needs to go, your endurance is increasing, and your strength is growing.

Similarly, God puts those who ask Him for more faith on a spiritual workout regimen, including a healthy diet of His Word, along with circumstances designed to make them trust Him more. The apostle Paul tells us that our faith increases by hearing the Word of God and having our minds transformed by it.[17] Likewise, Peter explains that God uses trials and testing to refine and mature our faith.[18]

Honestly, much of walking out a lifestyle of faith involves little more than mature responses and disciplining the mind. That is what Paul is driving at when he admonishes us to be vigilant, stand firm in our faith, and be courageous against the attacks that will come our way.[19]

That kind of faith takes perseverance. Persevering in your faith means "keeping on keeping on"—staying in the Word and prayer and continuing to make a good confession with your mouth day in and day out as you look expectantly for God's favor and goodness in every area of life. Just as a marathon runner only wins a grueling 26.2-mile race by enduring all the way to the finish line, so you will only win your destiny by walking out your faith through every season, looking to Jesus to strengthen you in your race. The prize will come after you endure.

---

17. See Romans 10:17; 12:2.
18. See 1 Peter 1:6–7.
19. See 1 Corinthians 16:13.

HE IS YOUR ABBA, FATHER

Friend, we are living in a day and age when the hearts of men and women are giving way to fear—and in the natural there certainly seems to be plenty of reason to fear. With the global economy in a state of flux, unrest and conflict filling our world, and uncertainty rampant in our own communities, it is no wonder that people are becoming distracted by fear and stress.

But it does not have to be that way with you! God has promised to be a loving heavenly Father in the worst of times, and to give you overcoming victory in every circumstance. The apostle John assures you that because you are part of God's family, you are constantly poised to overcome the world. *"And this is the victory that overcomes the world,"* he emphasized—*"our faith."*[20]

As His child you are an overcomer, and when the enemy tries to raise the specter of fear and dread in your life, you have the authority through the blood of Jesus to declare, "God has not given me the spirit of fear, but the spirit that empowers me to cry out Abba, Father." That Aramaic word *Abba* was a term of endearment and closeness that a child would use toward his father. The closest word we might have in English is "Daddy."

You see, God, your heavenly Father, is in a real way a Daddy to you, keeping you, protecting you, providing for you, and loving you deeply in a way not even the best earthly father could do. I know how much I love my own children, how I would lay down my very life to make sure they were protected, provided for, and that their futures were secure. It is a sobering thing to consider that God—our Abba, Father—loves us to a depth that no human father could love, to such an extent that we can go about our lives with the assurance that He will protect us, provide for us, and ensure our destinies, even as the rest of the world may fall apart.

---

20. 1 John 5:4.

> GOD'S WORD PROMISES THAT IN DUE SEASON,
> AS YOU CONTINUE TO STAND AND PERSEVERE,
> YOU WILL RECEIVE THE PRIZE YOU HAVE BEEN STANDING FOR.

DON'T LOSE CONFIDENCE!

I want to encourage you not to cast aside the fearless and bold confidence that brought you this far on the road to your destiny. God has said that your faith in Him—a faith that is confirmed and fortified by His Word—carries with it the promise of a great and rich reward. Your destiny in Him is waiting, a destiny that will continue to unfold in new and glorious chapters until the day you leave this earth for your heavenly home.

Do not faint! Do not let weariness, stress, or the temptation to fear stop you. God's Word promises that in due season, as you continue to stand and persevere, you will receive the prize. Continue claiming His promises. Continue thanking Him for every breakthrough and victory that comes your way. Continue asking Him for greater measures of faith.

Above all, ask Him for greater love for Him and His presence. Jesus said that if you keep on asking and pressing in, He will keep on giving in greater measure. I am confident of your victory!

YOU DON'T NEED TO PERFORM.
YOU JUST NEED TO BELIEVE.

FAVOR
TAKEAWAY

5

YOU ARE THE APPLE OF GOD'S EYE

Cassandra is a beautiful young woman who exudes confidence and purpose in everything she does. A marketing executive with a successful media firm, she regularly sets records for sales and has introduced a number of innovations that have helped her company exceed its performance and revenue expectations again and again.

It's not difficult to understand the reason for Cassandra's success. Not only does she reflect a positive, winning attitude, but the grace, kindness, and empathy with which she treats other people—from her clients and coworkers to her friends, family, and even strangers she meets—make it clear that she esteems others as valuable and worthwhile individuals. Her deportment causes people to trust and believe in Cassandra, and regularly opens doors that help her to further both her career and personal goals.

Amazingly, it wasn't always this way for Cassandra. In fact, for years, from the time she could first remember, Cassandra struggled with a low self-image, a severe lack of confidence, and a sense that she had little to offer that others would want. The foundation of this emotional handicap that held her back in school, hampered relationships, and kept her from succeeding in her employment was the severe criticism and abusive treatment she received at the hands of her mother from a very young age. Growing up in a home without a father, Cassandra and her younger siblings were at the mercy of a mother who suffered from wounds and emotional scars of her own and who took out her life's frustrations on her oldest daughter.

The verbal abuse and torment turned a young Cassandra, by character cheerful and full of joy, into a timid and fearful person who, by the time she was a young adult, could hardly look others in the eye and who was filled with self-hatred and a dread of the future. She was deeply distrustful and suspicious of every effort made by others to reach out and befriend her.

But then a miracle happened that turned Cassandra's life around, transforming her, little by little, back into the person God had created her to be—a victor and champion of life and success. At her church, a special guest speaker one Sunday morning talked about the ability of the heavenly Father to turn rejected, wounded individuals into winners, filling them with His confidence and boldness. "This lady spoke about God's desire to adopt each one of us into His joy-filled family," Cassandra recalled. "The words she spoke were right to me and my need, and made me feel deeply that God really wanted me—to love me, to change me, and to rearrange all the missing and broken parts."

"There was something else she said that stuck with me," Cassandra added.

She explained that each of us has the right, through a relationship with Jesus Christ, to be embraced as God's favorite child. She spoke about the children of Israel, and how God had picked them up out of slavery and bondage in Egypt, delivered them, and made them what this lady called the "apple of His eye." She said that meant they were the center of His attention, and He showered His goodness and love on Israel, not because of anything they had done, but because of His mercy.

I wanted that desperately. I wanted to be the apple of His eye. And even though I didn't know what it all meant, I decided then and there to make God my Father, to find out more about what He thought of me, and to embrace my place in His family.

As Cassandra began to spend time in God's Word, meditating on its truths, speaking them back to God, and declaring them over her circumstances, the miracle of a transformed life and destiny began to take hold. No, it didn't happen overnight, and even now Cassandra has setbacks and times when she has to refocus her attention on who she is—and who God is to her. But there is no going back, and Cassandra is moving every day in the goodness of God's mercy and faithfulness. She has chosen to embrace her place as God's favorite child.

A LOVE LETTER TO YOU

Now, as difficult as it might be for you to acknowledge it, just like Cassandra *you* can take your rightful place as God's favorite—as the apple of His eye. I am serious! As His child, redeemed through Jesus, you are the center of His attention. There is no one He would rather spend time with, and no one upon whom He would rather pour His prosperity and richest blessings, than you. Everything He has said overflows with expressions of love and provision for you, but you must take the time—and make the effort—to acknowledge, believe, and confess what He has promised. Just as Cassandra did, you must realign your thoughts and attitudes about who you are and who God is in your life.

Those promises are contained in Scripture—God's Word—where He invites you to "*behold*" the depth and extent of His love for you, a love so great He chose to adopt you into His family and call you His child.[1] In order to fully behold God's love, you have to make an effort to know Him in all of His fullness. God's Word is an extended love

---

1. 1 John 3:1.

letter straight to your heart, and the only way you will get to know the extent of His emotions and tenderness toward you is by immersing yourself in that love letter each and every day. That means spending time in His Word, meditating on His promises, and speaking them back to Him in prayer and worship.

That letter will tell you all about how He sent His Son to save you and how He has provided to meet every one of your needs, to heal and give you divine wholeness, to comfort you when you are sad or lonely, and to make a place of purpose and destiny for you in this world. It will tell you that He has a multitude of thoughts for you, and a plan and a purpose to prosper you. All this and more He spoke over you before the world was even formed, and those promises remain in place, just waiting for you to embrace them as your personal inheritance. Begin to saturate your mind and heart with His letter of love and purpose for you, reading it, listening to it, repeating the thoughts contained in it, reminding yourself and Him of them, and building yourself up daily with their truths.

Imagine a young man who is so head-over-heels in love with a young lady that he writes her multiple letters every day, explaining in detail the things he loves. He is smitten! He spares no emotion in pouring out his very heart to the lovely lady he hopes will one day be his bride.

Now just imagine that young woman receiving these precious notes in the mail—and carelessly tossing them aside unread. Think of the wonderful, intimate words of passion and care she would be missing out on, and think of the pained heart of the young man once he discovered that his carefully composed masterpieces of tenderness had been left unread!

Similarly, you are God's dear and beloved one, but if you never read the love letter He has so painstakingly crafted on your behalf, you will never come to fully know and appreciate all the things that He has done and prepared just for you. You will never understand His fiery and deep emotions for you, the jealousy that causes Him to want you all for Himself, with no one and nothing distracting from that intimacy.

> IF YOU NEVER READ THE LOVE LETTER HE HAS SO PAINSTAKINGLY CRAFTED ON YOUR BEHALF, YOU WILL NEVER COME TO FULLY KNOW AND APPRECIATE ALL THE THINGS THAT HE HAS DONE AND PREPARED JUST FOR YOU.

KNOWING—AND TAKING—YOUR PLACE

Believe me, there is a great need for God's people to come to this depth of understanding and revelation knowledge about who they are and about how much God desires to pour out His kingdom blessings upon them. He has a unique and wonderful plan of destiny for each of His children, but unless you truly believe and embrace that you are loved and cherished by Him, you could spend your entire life living beneath your best.

As a pastor, I don't believe I have ever seen people so uncertain about their identity, their motivation, and their purpose in life, as they are today. So many have been raised in broken and dysfunctional homes, where they weren't valued, validated, or perhaps even wanted. Their pursuits in life are so often based on a misguided attempt to prove their worth and to gain the esteem of others.

Others, like Cassandra, have been so beaten down by the disapproval and rejection of a parent, a spouse, or other loved one, that they cannot even reach the first rung on the ladder of life to pull themselves up. Instead they embrace the lie that they will never amount to anything—that they aren't smart enough, attractive enough, valued enough, or educated enough to embrace the destiny God created for them to enjoy.

Many are living day after day in a perpetual prison of shame, regret, and condemnation, not knowing that as God's children through Christ they can unlock the shackles of their past and truly embrace their place as God's favored one.

> YOU HAVE BEEN ADOPTED INTO GOD'S FAMILY,
> AND YOU CAN TAKE YOUR PLACE WITH BOLDNESS AND JOY.

Friend, I want you to consider for a moment the import of your position as God's child. He has declared that, just like the children of Israel whom He chose especially to bless and prosper so He could show His love to the world, so *you* are His chosen and beloved. In fact, you are an heir to all the grace, mercy, and provision He promised to Israel. You have been adopted into God's family, and you can take your place with boldness and joy.

TWISTS AND TURNS

The story of God's dealings with the children of Israel is filled with many twists and turns. Even though God chose them to be His special people, they did not receive the blessing easily. For starters, after living for hundreds of years as slaves in Egypt, they weren't eager to follow Moses into the vast unknown of the "Promised Land." They may have been mistreated by their Egyptian masters, but in their timidity they reasoned that at least in Egypt they knew what to expect!

It took a great deal for this fearful people to follow God's leading. Even though He promised to give them a land flowing with more than enough of everything they needed, they chose to listen to the fearful warnings of those who didn't trust God rather than the bold faith of those who confidently declared His promises. That doubt and fear led them into a forty-year detour during which God tested them, disciplined them, and prepared them for entrance to the land of promise.

Even after that, when they had gone in and taken possession of their inheritance, the years ahead were filled with many cycles of sin and rebellion, which ultimately brought more heartache as their disobedience led them into a long season of captivity at the hands of a bitter enemy.

You might think that all of this failure on the part of the people would have prompted God to throw in the towel and give up on the children of Israel. But that's not how God operates. At their lowest place, when they couldn't have been any less attractive or appealing to anyone, the great God of the universe spoke over them, recalling all the promises He had given them over the generations, and vowing to bring them back into His place of peace and prosperity.

HIS LOVE TOWARD YOU IS EVERLASTING

Are you like the children of Israel? Has your own history of following God been filled with twists and turns, and is your track record of faith less than stellar? Perhaps you started out strong, determined that you were going to receive in full all that God had promised, and fulfill your divine destiny. But little by little distractions set in, the call of the world grew strong, and in time you found yourself compromising in ways that eventually led you far from God and His plan for you. Perhaps today you are a mere shadow of the man or woman of God you once were, and your heart is filled with shame at how far you've fallen. Or maybe you haven't been sideswiped by such compromise, but the road has been long and you have begun to wonder if God really sees and understands.

The answer to your question is found in God's love letter to you, where, just as He did to Israel in their desperate hour, He declares to you, *"I have loved you with an everlasting love, therefore with lovingkindness I have drawn you."*[2]

Perhaps you weren't aware of this little secret of God's kingdom, but as one of His favored children—as the apple of His eye—you have a destiny that was secured even before you were born. Just as He spoke to Jeremiah, God declares that before you were formed inside of your mother, He knew you. In fact, more than that, He approved of you, set you apart, and had a blueprint for you, despite the background of your birth, your parents, or anything else.[3]

Furthermore, no matter the mistakes or missteps you may have made in life, that plan is still in operation and irrevocable, just as it was with the children of Israel. God says that His thoughts for you are good thoughts and His plans perfect and complete, to place you on a path where His goodness and mercy will chase you down. Your part in the plan is very simple: all you have to do is surrender to His process of guiding you into His destiny for you.

He wants you to trust in Him with all that is in you, and not to lean on your own intuition or understanding. It's possible that you already know the direction God is leading you, perhaps in ministry, in education, in business, in a profession, or in some other aspect of your life. But the long and sometimes painful process of *getting there* has caused you a lot of stress and uncertainty. It is precisely at that point that God is speaking to you in His still small voice: "I know the way. Just follow Me. Stop trying to figure the path out, and instead just enjoy the trip. I'll get you there."

Friend, the ongoing revelation of God's active desire and intent to open doors of purpose for you takes all the wind out of any lie the enemy or anyone else might have spoken over you that your background, your past, your abilities, your mistakes, or anything else can derail your divine destiny. God's thoughts toward you are so deep and

2. Jeremiah 31:3.
3. See Jeremiah 1:5.

countless, that the psalmist David says simply that they are *"more in number than the sand."*[4]

Now, here in South Florida, we have a lot of sand, and if you walk along a beach on the Atlantic coast and scan the horizon you will see miles and miles of it, as far as the eye can reach. Think about it! Every grain of those endless miles of sand represents a thought that God has for you, His favored child, and each one of those thoughts are actively focused on your peace, prosperity, and good.

Can you trust Him for the completion of that plan, the destiny He has for you? That, in all its simplicity, is what He wants from you: your surrender to Him of all your own plans apart from Him, along with your past, your failures, your sin, your brokenness and weakness, along with your absolute trust that He will perform His perfect plan in your life.

David counsels us not just to trust God, but to make Him our delight and obsession, and He, in turn, will fulfill all the desires of our heart. If we commit our way to Him, He promises to bring to pass the perfection of His destiny for us.

> IF WE COMMIT OUR WAY TO HIM, HE PROMISES TO BRING TO PASS THE PERFECTION OF HIS DESTINY FOR US.

PUSH *DELETE* ON YOUR FAULTS AND FAILURES

Now maybe you're thinking, "Henry, I've tried trusting God, and I never seem to be able to go very long before I fall. It's just too hard for me." Friend, the truth is that surrendering to the Lord and staying

4. Psalm 139:18.

in faith are part of the warfare to which God calls you as His favored child. Just as the children of Israel were forced to battle enemies and throw those enemies out of the Promised Land, in the same way God is calling you to do warfare against the doubt, fear, and unbelief that will assail you in your quest to embrace God's full destiny for you.

That means every time you fail or falter, you have an opportunity to take a step ahead and gain more ground from the enemy by quickly turning away from your failure, repenting, and putting it under the blood of Jesus, pressing *delete* on the condemnation the devil tries to throw at you, and pressing ahead in trusting God. It is all part of the transforming process God is doing in your life on a daily basis.

In the next chapter we will take a close look at one of the key ways you can strengthen your inner person and consistently choose faith over fear—and God's mercy and peace over condemnation and guilt—by renewing your mind with the truths of God's Word. They will guide you in your quest for His best, bring you consistent assurance of His love and care, and keep you from being derailed by the enemy's lies.

YOU ARE FAVORED
BECAUSE YOU ARE GOD'S FAVORITE.

FAVOR
TAKEAWAY

6

REDEEMING YOUR THOUGHTS, RENEWING YOUR MIND

If you have spent any amount of time on a laptop or computer, you have likely had a run-in viruses, malware, worms, spyware, and the like. They go by different names, they work in different ways, and their functions may vary, but they all serve one purpose: to infect your computer, put it under the control of someone else, and even corrupt its memory beyond repair. In order to defend yourself from such attacks, it is necessary to arm your computer with a veritable arsenal of firewalls and sophisticated software designed to inoculate against an unseen army of online hackers and malicious attackers determined to infiltrate, control, and even destroy your computer's electronic brain and all your important files.

Computer experts say that to effectively battle these unseen and unrelenting enemies, you must be on constant guard, keeping your anti-virus software up-to-date and steering clear of websites that may hide malware or other infections. Yet even the most vigilant of persons may still find themselves the victim of a destructive cyber-attack. I personally know of many individuals who have unwittingly opened themselves up to such assaults, and found their computers completely overwhelmed by malicious infections. At that point the only remedy is to have their computer's hard drive completely wiped of all its memory. Pretty drastic!

GARBAGE IN, GARBAGE OUT

Just like the malicious infections that stalk your computer, there are an overwhelming host of malicious weapons the enemy of your soul has let loose in an effort to infect your mind with thoughts and distractions that will take you far from God's destiny for you. Think about it for a moment! Sitting right in the middle of your home is a television set ready to spew out over you and your family every imaginable and wicked depiction of immorality, pride, anger, violence, and selfishness. The average American spends between thirty and forty hours a week in front of the television,[1] and guess what? A majority of what they are watching is not wholesome and uplifting, but rather full of scenes and images that compromise their thoughts and imaginations.

Or how about your computer? Nearly every American today has access to the online world through computers, laptops, iPads, tablets, and smartphones. Consumption of Internet media continues to skyrockets. Millions of people spend untold hours a day surfing the web and, in the process, being exposed to temptations that can destroy their lives. One study estimated that up to 30 percent of the Internet traffic today involves some sort of pornography,[2] and one watchdog group warns that there are over four million pornographic websites on the Internet—the majority built and maintained by online predators who are constantly on the prowl for people they can draw into their

---

1. John Koblin, "How Much Do We Love TV? Let Us Count the Ways," *New York Times*, June 30, 2016, https://www.nytimes.com/2016/07/01/business/media/nielsen-survey-media-viewing.html?_r=0 (accessed June 14, 2017).
2. Patrick Craine, "30% of web's total traffic is for porn," Lifesite.com, April 12, 2012, http://www.lifesitenews.com/news/30- of-webs-total-traffic-is-for-porn-tech-magazine (accessed March 3, 2017).

web of filth and immorality.[3] If you or your family are regularly on the Internet, it's only a matter of time before you will be confronted by this evil.

Likewise, the radio, music, magazines, and other media are assaulting people as never before with images, ideas, innuendos, thoughts, and suggestions that are absolutely at odds with God's purposes of righteousness and wholeness. Sadly, the majority of people today have no understanding of the destructive purposes of the enemy. They are putting garbage into their minds, and garbage is what is coming out. For you, friend, it means that many of the conversations you have with others at school, on the job, and elsewhere are all likely to be tinged with things that the enemy can use to infect your mind and pull you away from God's truth as your guide and compass.

IT'S ALL IN YOUR MIND

The world today, with all its various philosophies and appealing alternatives to God's kingdom, exerts a powerful pull on individuals looking for something to satisfy them and give them meaning and purpose. God likens the enemy of our souls to a predatory lion, always searching for those he can attack and destroy.[4] And the most vulnerable point of attack for most people is their minds, the place of their innermost thoughts, desires, and emotions. Until a person surrenders his or her life to Christ, turns to His truth, and allows God to transform his or her mind and thoughts to mirror His, that person will continue to be vulnerable to the deception and attacks of the enemy.

No one is exempt. Living in this world automatically makes you vulnerable to the attacks of the enemy. No matter how hard you try to resist him, without God's transforming power and protection you are going to be influenced by the malicious attacks and infectious viruses of lies, sin, and evil that the devil throws against you—particularly in

---

3. See "Porn on the Web," TopTenReviews.com, http://internet-filter-review. toptenreviews.com/internet-pornography-statistics.html (accessed March 3, 2017).
4. 1 Peter 5:8.

your mind. What you have taken in with your eyes over the years—the thoughts you have dwelled upon, the choices you have made, and even the words that others have spoken over you—all take their toll on your life, and on the destiny that God has planned for you. The "hard drive" of your mind has been corrupted by the things of this world, and it is going to take a work of God's grace and power to wipe your mind clean of the enemy's "malware" of evil, and to turn your thoughts back to God's truth.

Full surrender to God means giving Him access to every corner of who you are, including your mind with all of its imaginations, ideas, thoughts, and emotions. When you fully surrender your mind to the transforming power of the Holy Spirit—that part of God's person who dwells deep inside you and shows you the way—He will replace the enemy's thoughts and lies with His truth and righteousness.

Yes, God wants to redeem your thoughts and renew your mind, but He won't do it without your involvement. As I have said before, God has by far the major part to play in making you who He planned you to become, and in unfolding your dreams and destiny. But you have a crucial role in the process as well. You can't do God's part, and He won't do yours.

YOU CAN'T DO GOD'S PART, AND HE WON'T DO YOURS.

Friend, whenever God gives a command, you can be sure that He will empower you to fulfill that command and be victorious. Your part is simply to surrender to His will and allow Him, by His Holy Spirit, to give you victory. As God's child you are called to present yourself—body, soul, and spirit—to Him, and be transformed through His Word. God's Word, the Bible, is the sole source of life-changing truth that God has provided to transform your mind, wipe it clean of all the worldly and wicked thoughts that guided and controlled you before you became His child, and replace those thoughts with His thoughts.

God tells us that those who have not come to faith in Christ cannot understand the things of God, but when we have His Spirit living within us we are empowered to understand His truth and to be changed by it. God commands us as His children to be *"transformed"* by the renewing of our minds through His powerful and life-changing Word.[5] As we submit to the process of being changed by God's Word, the transformation is almost miraculous in its impact.

> AS WE SUBMIT TO THE PROCESS OF BEING CHANGED BY GOD'S WORD, THE TRANSFORMATION IS ALMOST MIRACULOUS IN ITS IMPACT.

SUBMIT TO HIS WORD

Charles had been a Christian for just a few months, and while he loved the Lord and had a genuine desire to grow in His faith, he was finding himself beginning to revert to some of the attitudes and thoughts that had plagued him before he gave his life to Christ. Old issues of anger, lust, selfishness, pride, and fear, along with sinful desires he thought had disappeared when he committed his life to Christ, came flooding back into his heart and mind, causing him confusion and condemnation.

---

5. Romans 12:2.

"What's wrong with me?" Charles asked his pastor. "Am I even a Christian anymore? How can I be the person God has called me to be when I can't even get rid of these old sins?"

Charles' pastor explained to him that even though he had been saved from sin and was indeed, a *"new creation"* in Christ Jesus, his old habits and attitudes wouldn't simply dissolve.[6] They had to be replaced by new thought patterns—thoughts anchored in the eternal truths of God's Word.

"Charles, you need to reprogram your mind by spending time every day reading and thinking on God's Word, and declaring it back to Him in prayer," Charles' pastor explained. "If you will give yourself to the Word of God just like you used to give yourself to other things, I guarantee that those thoughts will fade and be replaced by God's peace and victory."

Charles did just that, and slowly but surely the old thought patterns the enemy had used to control his life for so long faded, and were replaced by a quiet assurance from the heavenly Father. "I realized that, just as Scripture says, the Word of God is powerful to renew my mind and mold and conform my thoughts to His purposes," Charles said. "I asked God to give me a love for His Word, to help me understand and make it a part of my life, and He did just that. The change in me has been miraculous."

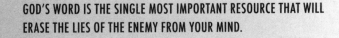

GOD'S WORD IS THE SINGLE MOST IMPORTANT RESOURCE THAT WILL ERASE THE LIES OF THE ENEMY FROM YOUR MIND.

---

6. 2 Corinthians 5:17.

FAITH COMES THROUGH HEARING

In a previous chapter we established the importance of faith in the lives of those who wish to grow into all that God intended them to be. We found that it is impossible to move ahead in our quest for His destiny in our lives without it. We have to believe that He is the only one who can change us, and that He will richly reward our efforts to know Him and His ways.[7] Seeing faith and full dependence upon Him blossom and increase in His children is the one thing above all others that brings God joy, and He has provided an incomparable resource to get faith inside of us.

But where does faith come from? In his letter to the Romans, the apostle Paul tells us that faith in God comes by being fully engaged in His Word.[8] That's right! Once again, God's Word—the Bible—is the single most important resource that will erase the lies of the enemy from your mind, and replace them with God's powerful truth.

I'm not trying to say that erasing those lies is easy. As a pastor I am often brought face-to-face with men and women who have come out of pasts of great darkness and misery. The lifestyles and actions which they were involved in for years have seared their minds with condemnation and regret. Even though they have taken the gift of forgiveness and salvation that God freely offers, the enemy continues to taunt them. "You can't just let go of who you were back then," he'll say. "It's not that easy. You've done some terrible things. Don't think you can just leave them behind. You'll suffer for your past the rest of your life."

Others have suffered horrific abuse—verbal, physical, emotional, and worse—from a parent or other trusted adult, and now the memories of what they faced years and decades ago are like red-hot brands burning into their minds. Some have been told repeatedly that they are worthless, useless, or stupid, and will never amount to anything.

7. See Hebrews 11:6.
8. See Romans 10:17.

Although they have by faith received salvation and healing from Christ, they are having a very difficult time leaving those lies behind and living in the destiny God has purposed for them.

Each time I hear these stories, while I share in their pain and heartache, I also know that they have at their fingertips a weapon that will empower them to destroy the lies the devil uses to attack them. It is God's Word, and in it they will find a very different outlook about themselves than the lies they have been told. In it, they will find a destiny waiting for them that far outshines the abuse and misery of their pasts. God's outlook will destroy the darkness of the enemy because it is based on absolute light, truth, and righteousness—before which all the lies of the enemy crumble.

Yes, your heavenly Father is filled with kindness, gentleness, forgiveness, and purpose for all who come to Him for help. You can be totally assured that if you turn to Him, all the old things of your life will pass away and will be replaced with the new. Through Jesus Christ, God will powerfully mold you into a new creature and position you to receive the destiny and inheritance He originally created you to enjoy.

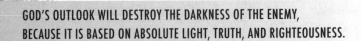

GOD'S OUTLOOK WILL DESTROY THE DARKNESS OF THE ENEMY, BECAUSE IT IS BASED ON ABSOLUTE LIGHT, TRUTH, AND RIGHTEOUSNESS.

REPROGRAMMING YOUR MIND

This is great news. But the enemy has a way of stealing our treasure away from us through distractions, disappointments, and accusations. Unless the truth of God's Word is being reinforced daily in our lives, we are prone to drift away from our destiny. Your thoughts must be redeemed, your mind renewed—programmed and updated like your computer's hard drive, if you will—through God's Word. The faith that you first received must be fed on a *daily* basis, and the only way to nourish and grow your faith is through staying in God's Word—reading and hearing it; thinking, meditating, and praying about it; and declaring it over your life. Let's take a closer look at those three elements.

READING AND HEARING THE WORD

The sum total of God's wisdom and counsel for your life is contained in His Word, the Bible. It tells you who you are as His child and what you are called to do in His kingdom. Jesus said that in order to truly follow Him, it is crucial for you to stay in His Word, and as you spend time getting to know Him in this way, you will know the truth and it will make you free.[9] In fact, Jesus referred to Himself as *"the way, the truth, and the life."*[10] That is a powerful statement, and it goes to the heart of how your mind is renewed through His Word. You see, *truth* cannot change you until it gets inside you and becomes a revelation in your *mind* and *heart*. When God's truth becomes a revelation to you it engages your faith, giving you boldness and authority to believe and grab on to the things of God—healing, prosperity, transformation, destiny. The transforming power of God's Word will steer you in the right direction in every area of your life.

But the only way you can know the truth is by engaging and interacting with it. That means giving yourself to God's Word through reading it, studying it, listening to messages about it—in short, saturating yourself in the truth. When you soak your mind in God's Word, you will find yourself thinking God's thoughts, declaring His promises, and acting like God's man or woman.

---

9. See John 8:32.
10. John 14:6.

THINKING ON, MEDITATING ON, AND PRAYING GOD'S WORD

When He left this earth to go back to the Father, Jesus promised to send the Holy Spirit to lead us into God's truth. The Holy Spirit is the key person in your relationship with God, because He will take what you have read and heard from God's Word and make it powerful and life-changing to you. As you read and take in God's Word, it is important to think about what it means, reflect on how you should respond to it, ask the Holy Spirit to make God's truth real and powerful to you, and actually take Scripture and pray it back to God. In my own life I have found great power when I speak God's truth back to Him. Something powerful happens when I converse with the Father about the truths His Holy Spirit has revealed to me from His Word. The same will happen to you. As you speak truth from God's Word back to Him, that Word will become a revelation deep inside you that will change you and lead you further into receiving the fullness of His inheritance. When that begins to happen, your prayers change into declarations.

DECLARING GOD'S WORD OVER YOUR CIRCUMSTANCES

This declaration phase is the next step in building faith, because it is at this point that the Word gains dramatic, overcoming power in your life. You see, God's Word is eternal and living. It has no beginning or end. It is absolute truth that exists independent of time and experience. But it is also powerful to break into your circumstances, your attitudes, and your past, and to destroy any lie of the enemy that has you enchained.

But in order for that to happen, His Word must become personal and vital in you. When you declare God's truth about yourself, your destiny, and the inheritance you have in Him, you are going to that next step of faith.

WHEN YOU DECLARE GOD'S TRUTH ABOUT YOURSELF,
YOUR DESTINY, AND THE INHERITANCE YOU HAVE IN HIM,
YOU ARE GOING TO THAT NEXT STEP OF FAITH.

REPROGRAMMING IN ACTION

Here's how it works. God's Word declares that you are a new creation through Christ. As you contemplate that truth in your mind, begin to talk to the Father about it. "Thank You, Lord, for making me a new creation through Jesus," you might say. "I believe it, I take it by faith, and I ask You to show me how You are changing me and making me into the person You created me to be."

Now, as that simple truth begins to take hold, the next thing is to take a step of faith and make it a declaration in your life. "I am a new creation in Christ," you declare. "The old has passed away, the new has come. I am no longer the person that I once was. Jesus has taken it all away and made me new. I am a child of God with all the rights, authority, and inheritance that God says I have. I am going to learn what those are, I am going to press in, and I am going to become all that God has created me to be—because I am a new creation. The Word of God is changing me from the inside out."

Do you understand what is happening here? Your mind, your thoughts, your attitudes, and your words are lining up with God's eternal truth—His Word. Friend, there is no power anywhere that can come against you when you are in agreement with God's Word. When you declare His thoughts over your life, your destiny, your past, present, and future, along with your family and loved ones, you are covered and complete!

The Word of God is vast, and every page has promises for you to claim and declare. As you take time to mine the depths of its wisdom you will be amazed at how your thoughts are redeemed, your mind renewed, and your destiny forged. Here are just a few of the declarations you can make, based on what God says about who you are in Christ:

- I am the righteousness of God in Christ.[11]

- I am seated in heavenly places with Christ Jesus.[12]

- I can come boldly into God's throne room and receive help for every need—physical, emotional, relational, financial—in every area of life.[13]

- God will supply every need I have according to His riches in Christ Jesus.[14]

- I was created for good works, to fulfill God's kingdom here on earth.[15]

- God has a great plan to prosper me and fulfill His purpose in me.[16]

- I have been chosen by God, and through Him I am holy and loved.[17]

These are just a handful of the truths God has declared over you. The Scriptures are loaded with others every bit as powerful. The more that you embrace and declare who you are in Christ, the more you will clean out the old patterns of thoughts and lies that the enemy has used to control and manipulate you, and the more those will be replaced with the absolute, timeless truth of who God says you are, and what He says He has for you.

---

11. See 2 Corinthians 5:21.
12. See Ephesians 2:6.
13. See Hebrews 4:16.
14. See Philippians 4:19.
15. See Ephesians 2:10.
16. See Jeremiah 29:11.
17. See Ephesians 1:4.

FEED ON THE TRUTH

A wise father once used this illustration to explain the process of God's transforming power to his young son. "There are two wolves at war within your heart, son," the father said. "One is moved by kindness, wisdom, and mercy, while the other one is controlled by anger, cruelty, and hatred. Only one can be in control of your heart and mind, and the one that controls you will influence the direction you go in life." The boy thought for a moment and then asked, "How do I know which one will win?" The father replied, "The one you feed will win, and the one you starve will die."

Friend, the same goes for you in your heart life. Which wolf are you feeding? Your destiny depends upon it. If you will give God's Word preeminence in your daily thoughts, and allow Him to clean and rewrite your mental hard drive with His thoughts and truths, you can put to flight every wicked influence and lie of the enemy.

Your mind is the major battlefield upon which you will meet the enemy of your destiny. The circumstances you face, the actions and attitudes of others, the adversity that seems to hold you back—all of these issues are secondary to how you fare in the battle for your mind. God has empowered you through His Word to take back the territory the enemy has stolen through the lies that have made you fearful. God commands you to *take every thought captive* under Christ's headship in your life.[18]

In the next chapter we will see how God's Word equips us to stand and fight the enemy on his turf, and win the prize of God's destiny for us.

---

18. 2 Corinthians 10:5 ESV.

GOD'S WORD NEVER SITS STILL IN YOUR HEART.
IT ALWAYS TRANSFORMS YOU.

FAVOR
TAKEAWAY

7

STAND AND FIGHT

Have you ever seen a bully in action? Bullies don't pick on the strong and confident. They go for the meek and timid, those who are the least likely to fight back and defend themselves. That's because, for the most part, bullies are themselves weak and cowardly, and will back down if their position is challenged. Their strategy against a victim is almost entirely built on intimidation. Once somebody calls his bluff, the game is up and the bully usually turns tail and runs away.

Friend, in your march to God's full destiny there is a bully who is tracking your every move, looking for an opening to try to intimidate you and block your spiritual blessing. He is, of course, the devil, and while people by and large fear him as a powerful force to be reckoned with, the truth is that you, as a child of the Most High God, have nothing to dread. This enemy is already a defeated foe because you have the blood of Jesus and the Word of God, and those are weapons before which Satan has no power. Satan is dreadfully afraid of Jesus, because He knows that the Son of the living God has completely defeated him and he is headed for eternal destruction. Under the lordship of Jesus you are a victor against all the wiles of the devil.

Remember, against the child of God the only resources this enemy has are lies, and like any bully he can only rely on intimidation and deceit to try to manipulate and control people. Sadly, far too many of God's children continue to be deceived by this liar, and live their lives in fear, poverty, sickness, and despair because they do not realize that they have the authority to defeat this powerless foe.

If that is where you are living right now, I am here to assure you that the enemy's days of victory and manipulation in your life are over—if you choose. You have the power and the authority to kick the devil out of your circumstances and your destiny. In the area of your health, finances, relationships, career, and anything else that the enemy has stolen, it is time for you to stand up, fight, and win the victory for now and forever. Let's find out how!

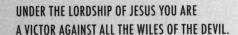

UNDER THE LORDSHIP OF JESUS YOU ARE
A VICTOR AGAINST ALL THE WILES OF THE DEVIL.

CONFRONTING THE LIES

Ever since he was a kid, Steve had been picked on mercilessly. Because he didn't have any close friends and was by nature shy and timid, kids in his tough neighborhood got used to walking all over him, stealing from him, pushing him around, and beating him up. Steve just faced the abuse as a normal part of his life, something he had to accept. But as he got older—and bigger—he began to resent the name-calling, the teasing, the pranks, and the other abuse at his expense that the kids around him seemed to take as their right.

One day on his way home from school, thirteen-year-old Steve began to be followed by a couple of the neighborhood boys who were used to terrorizing and threatening him. Steve quickly ducked down an alley to try to avoid their inevitable attack, but the two were on him instantly—and they began to push him around and demand money.

As Steve began to give in to the thugs, he recalled the countless other times that he had been beaten up, hurt, and robbed by bullies. Indignation and anger rose up within him. Before he really knew what he was doing, Steve turned and challenged the two boys, and when one of the thugs began to use a little muscle, Steve responded in kind, throwing a quick right that decked the bully and sent the other boy falling backward in shock. As Steve raised his fists to defend himself—something he had never even considered before—the boy on the ground slowly got up in rage, saw Steve prepared to put up a fight, backed off with a menacing stare, and then turned and walked quickly away, followed by his sidekick.

Steve was as shocked as the bullies that he had stood his ground—and won. And while a few of the neighborhood toughs tested Steve's mettle over the next few weeks, it wasn't long before Steve had gained a new reputation. Where he had once been terrorized into submission and was quick to give in to threats, now he walked his neighborhood with quiet confidence and a countenance that made it clear he would not back down to intimidation.

Maybe, in a spiritual sense, you recognize a little of Steve in yourself. The enemy has had you intimidated for years, filling you with fear over the future, shame over your past, condemnation over a lifestyle that once had you bound, or even agony over a sinful habit or activity you still struggle with.

Maybe you're sick, and the devil has you convinced that you will stay ill, even though Jesus has paid for your healing and divine health. Maybe you have lived in poverty or financial lack for years through being unemployed or underemployed, and the devil has you convinced that, despite what God's Word says about your being the head and not the tail,[1] despite God's promise that He will supply all your needs according to His riches in glory,[2] you are condemned to a lifestyle of second-bests, hand-me-downs, and leftovers. Maybe you have been persuaded by the words of others that you will never succeed or reach the dream of destiny that you have carried in your heart for years.

These are the lies that the devil has used against men and women just like you since the beginning of time. And like Steve with his neighborhood bullies, many of God's own people give the enemy the power to push them around and limit their future. They have been convinced that the lies of the devil are more relevant in their lives than God's Word.

But just as Steve found that the intimidation and threats of the bullies in his life had been nothing more than bluff and bluster, you are about to discover that what the enemy has been telling you about your past, present, and future is nothing more than empty lies designed to intimidate you into submission to his evil and destructive purposes. And when you get a full revelation of the real truth—that you are a child of God with authority and power to kick the devil and his minions back into the pit—things are going to change drastically for you.

Now hear me well—you have no such power and authority on your own. Without the finished work of Calvary, the blood of the Lamb, and the Word of God in your life, the devil really does have the power to push your buttons. You really are headed for abject failure without Jesus as the Lord of your life, and the enemy of your soul really is a dangerous foe—if you have allowed him access.

But if God is charting your course and defending you, it doesn't matter how much firepower of wickedness the enemy has at his disposal, because the smallest hint of God's power through Jesus is sufficient to send the devil packing.

---

1. See Deuteronomy 28:13.
2. See Philippians 4:19.

> YOUR HEAVENLY FATHER IS POWERFUL TO SAVE, AND ALL YOU HAVE TO DO
> IS STAND STILL AND ALLOW HIM TO FIGHT FOR YOU.

STAND STILL AND SEE; MOVE AHEAD AND LIVE

You no doubt know well the story of the Exodus of the children of Israel from the bondage of slavery in Egypt—which is a type and forecast of the bondage out of which Christ saves each of us. God specifically prepared His chosen people Israel for a great angelic assault that was to come upon the godless kingdom of Egypt, during which all the firstborn of that land would be killed—except those who had protected their families by placing blood over their doorposts. When the angel of death swept through the land that night, he *passed over* all the families of Israel.

The children of Israel were released by Pharaoh, only to be pursued by the Egyptian army after Pharaoh changed his mind. As the children of Israel fled, they soon found their way blocked by the Red Sea. They could not go forward, because the vast sea stood in their way, but if they stayed where they were, they faced certain annihilation at the hands of the powerful and terrifying Egyptian army. It was at this time of almost certain destruction that God spoke a word to them, commanding them through Moses to *"fear ye not, stand still, and see the salvation of the LORD."*[3] God went on to tell them that He would fight for them in this place of danger and death, and all they had to do was watch Him gain the victory for them.

The same goes for you in your own circumstances. Perhaps there have been life experiences that have held you back from reaching your goals and dreams. Maybe you have felt that you are in bondage to your past, to a failed relationship, to past mistakes and failures. Maybe the

---

3. Exodus 14:13 KJV.

words of others have held you back. Whatever it is that has held you in bondage and kept you frozen in fear, intimidation, or mediocrity, you have a champion in your corner who will fight for you! You are not condemned to struggle through on your own, to live in defeat. Your heavenly Father is powerful to save, and all you have to do is stand still and allow Him to fight for you.

It is important to note, however, that after telling them to "stand still" God commanded the children of Israel to "move forward" into victory. Had they stayed where they were, they would have been sitting targets for the wrath of the Egyptian forces. It was only as God parted the waters of the Red Sea and the children of Israel moved ahead into the path God had made for them that they could make their way safely from their enemy.

As God's children moved through the way made for them in the Red Sea, their enemy was in hot pursuit. But as the last of the Israelites made it to the other side, the Egyptian army was still pounding across the sand in the middle of the Red Sea. God called the sea back over them and brought great calamity upon them. What had been a way of escape for Israel became a place of destruction for their enemy.

Friend, God knows that in your own strength, you are no match for the power of the enemy. In this world, without the mercy and help of God, there is reason to fear. But with God on your side, the enemy's tactics become nothing more than hollow threats and baseless intimidation, and, like the children of Israel, you can move ahead with confidence and faith.

THERE WERE GIANTS TO FACE

Not long after that mighty victory, God called the children of Israel to go in and take the land that He had promised them as an inheritance. God specified that the enemies the children of Israel would face would be greater and stronger than they were, and in their own power they could have no chance to defeat them and take their inheritance. However, He also told them that He would go before them, and with His might and power, no one and no thing could stand before them.

God Himself had commissioned them to clean out the Promised Land, and He promised to go before them as a *"consuming fire"*[4] to enable them to destroy the enemies quickly, go in, and possess the land. Of course, you would think that having just witnessed God's delivering hand in destroying the Egyptian army on their behalf, the children of Israel would have jumped at the opportunity for this new adventure to which God was calling them. After all, He promised to give them the victory—all they had to do was trust and obey.

But fear can be a paralyzing factor, and if you don't confront it head-on with the Word of God and faith, you will find yourself at its mercy. When Moses sent in twelve scouts to spy out the land, ten of the spies came back intimidated and fearful. Yes, they said, the land was brimming with abundance—*"milk and honey,"*[5] as Scripture puts it—and it would certainly be a great place to live. Nonetheless, they warned, the land was also filled with giants and there would be no way they could conquer it. It was hopeless! The giants that lived in the Promised Land were just too strong!

Fear had conquered the hearts of those ten spies. In their minds, God's promise had become hopeless. Friend, "hopeless" is the curse that too many people are living under today. Maybe you're one of those people. The problems in your life seem too great. You're afraid of failure. There are giants of intimidation, of past failures, sins, and addictions that are just too great for you to achieve the destiny that is meant for your life. *It's hopeless*, you think. That is the lie the enemy uses to hold men and women back for a lifetime.

But it doesn't have to be that way. There was another report, given by two lone brave scouts, Joshua and Caleb. They had seen the same things the other twelve witnessed, the *"milk and honey"* abundance,

---

4. Deuteronomy 4:24.
5. Numbers 13:27.

along with the imposing giants. But they also knew what God had said, they recalled how He had delivered them at the Red Sea crossing, and their report was one of faith and courage. "Don't listen to this talk of fear and failure," they no doubt shouted to Moses and the people of God. "Let us go up at once and possess the land God has promised us! For with God's power and authority behind us, we are well able to defeat these giants and take the land!"

Which group would you go with, the ten or the two? Which group had the power, authority, drive, ambition, faith, and confidence to win? That's right, Caleb and Joshua had the fire within—the Holy Spirit fire—and there is no doubt that God was pleased with their confession.

So which opinion did the children of Israel go with? Well, not only did they disregard the faithful report of Joshua and Caleb, but they actually wanted to *kill* these two courageous warriors for insisting that the army of God could succeed against the giants. In the end, all of Israel ignored the will of God, the promise of His help, and the land of prosperity and plenty waiting for them. Instead, they embraced fear, doubt, and unbelief, and paid a dreadful price. For the next forty years the children of Israel wandered in the wilderness within just a few miles of the land that was to be theirs.

None of that doubting, fearful generation lived to enter into the Promised Land—except two lone, faithful men: Joshua and Caleb. God honored their willingness to believe Him at all costs, and though they were old men, they were still strong and able-bodied when God actually let Israel enter the Promised Land, and they gladly received their inheritance. The others died and were buried just outside the border of the land God wanted to give them.

WHOSE REPORT WILL YOU BELIEVE?

How about you, my friend and fellow child of God? Whose report will you believe? Will you allow the enemy to bully you with lies that you can't succeed, that you can't be healed, that you'll never graduate from college, start a business, overcome an addiction, or achieve some dream that you've held in your heart? In your own power, of course, he is right. You can't succeed if all you have is your own abilities.

But you aren't operating in that realm any more. You have the God of all power and mercy on your side. Accept nothing less in your life than the report of the Lord—a report of victory in every circumstance, a report of prosperity and abundance, a report of success and achievement. Yes, just like the children of Israel, you are destined to face giants of adversity and challenge throughout your life. They will always be there to confront you, trying to intimidate you into taking less than God's best for you. Your response to those challenges is crucial to reaching the fullness of God's destiny for you. Will you identify with the ten spies who allowed fear and unbelief to block them from reaching their Promised Land? Or will you side with Caleb and Joshua and stare down the bullies that try to intimidate you?

Friend, I believe you are like Caleb. You are like Joshua.

You see giants, and you trust instead of run.

You are a fighter—and a winner.

YOU ARE STRONGER THAN YOU THINK.

FAVOR
TAKEAWAY

8

STEPPING FORWARD INTO GOD'S FULLNESS

The world is in need of men and women who are filled with God's Spirit, His Word, and the faith to battle the giants that are coming. You see, there are too many people who will go just so far before fear and uncertainty intimidate them. They talk the talk, but when faced with real life adversity that stretches their faith, they turn tail and run in fear.

Meanwhile, standing in the shadow are the few, the unnoticed, those who have been prepared in the lonely wilderness of isolation and affliction, who have been seasoned with trials and can now step forward, as did a shepherd boy named David, and destroy the giants that terrorize.

RUN TOWARD YOUR ENEMY

Recall how David spent his youth keeping sheep far from the eyes of other people, a world away from the high-profile life God would later usher him into as the king of Israel. As he sat out under the stars or under the blazing sun, communing with his heavenly Father, making up songs of praise, and meditating on the greatness and majesty of his

God, he would be confronted from time to time with dangers unique to his situation, like bears and lions that came out of the wild to kill the sheep.

In this lonely and isolated arena David learned how to trust God and how to respond in faith and courage. These were small beginnings, a simple apprenticeship program that God had David under as He prepared this future warrior and champion for the day when he would face much bigger obstacles.

As you remember, that day arrived when David was called by his father, Jesse, to take provisions to David's brothers, who were serving under King Saul, fighting the Philistines. When David arrived at the encampment of Saul's army, he was confronted with a sight that filled him with righteous indignation. Standing on a hillside was a big and ugly giant, fully armed and imposing, taunting the army of Israel and challenging them to come out and fight him. But instead of running out to meet this enemy of God, Saul's army cringed in fear as they caught a glimpse of this nine-foot-tall mountain of a man intimidating them with his arrogance.

Now get the picture. Here is Saul's army of trained and well-equipped warriors who have God on their side. But instead of trusting in Him and running out to defeat this bragging enemy, they cower in fear, convinced that Goliath is mightier than they are. Into this disgraceful scene steps the youthful David, who turns to the soldiers and wonders aloud: "*Who is this uncircumcised Philistine, that he should defy the armies of the living God?*"[1]

Naturally, such a bold stance of faith-filled courage didn't sit well with the fearful soldiers, and one of them—David's own brother—ripped into him for his stand, accusing David of pride and of just wanting to have a front-row seat to a violent battle.

Friend, be aware that in your decision to stand in faith and courage against the giants in your life, you might be surprised at those

---

1. 1 Samuel 17:26.

who oppose you. Quite likely, some of that opposition will come from the very individuals you would have expected to be your advocates and partners in faith—fellow believers you thought were traveling the same road. But not everyone chooses the hard road of faith and perseverance against an enemy. You see, it is far easier to be a part of the crowd of mediocrity and passivity than to stand and contend with a foe who appears impossible to defeat. In fact, as you fight for your destiny, you may find yourself with not a single other human ally—but only God's Spirit assuring you of His presence and help.

I am sure as he stood there watching Goliath on the hillside spouting his wickedness, while Saul's fear-filled soldiers stared at him in anger because of his God-confidence, David had fleeting thoughts of just turning around and running back to his sheep in the wilderness. It certainly would have been far easier. But God doesn't call His people to their destinies through easy circumstances. David was destined to be king, and the road to his throne began with confronting the giant Goliath. Likewise, your destiny will be secured only through confronting your own personal giants.

Scripture recounts that all David took with him into the battle against Goliath was his sling and five stones that he had selected out of a nearby brook. But we know that David was armed with far more than a slingshot. He had the power and authority of almighty God covering him. While the giant was arrayed in all his battle gear, and stood to face David with self-assurance and bravado, David staked his victory on one declaration: *"I come to you in the name of the LORD of hosts, the God of the armies of Israel, whom you have defied."*[2]

Friend, I challenge you to make similar bold declarations against the giants that come against you in your God-ordained quest for your destiny and purpose. You serve the same God, you have been anointed with kingdom purpose, and you have been empowered by God's Holy Spirit. Most importantly, you have the name of Jesus—with all that name implies—as the foundation for your authority. It is an authority

---

2. 1 Samuel 17:45.

that empowers you to declare against doubt, fear, unbelief, addictions, condemnation, shame, or any other barriers to your full inheritance in Christ: "I come against you in the name of Jesus, the name of above every name, and I demand that you get out of my way and hinder me no more in my destiny."

There is something else David did as he confronted the giant Goliath that was a bold statement of faith and confidence in God. Selecting one of the stones and placing it in his sling, David ran— yes, *ran!*—toward Goliath with his sling whirling above his head. He didn't take time to size up the enemy, nor did he spend time dodging and weaving trying to get the right advantage. He already had all the advantage he needed. He raced toward the giant fully confident that victory was his. And at just the opportune moment, Goliath no doubt lifting his huge spear to kill the boy who dared come out against him, David released the stone. It streaked through the air and embedded itself into the forehead of Goliath with such force that the sound echoed throughout the valley.

Can you imagine the deathly silence as both armies breathlessly watched Goliath, the mighty warrior of the Philistines, totter for a few seconds then fall with a metallic clatter at the feet of the victorious shepherd boy? The next sound was the deafening cheer of victory from the army of Saul as the soldiers suddenly realized their worst nightmare had just been felled by a simple young man with a big faith in God.

CONFRONTING YOUR GIANTS

The giants you face in life may not be nine feet tall with armor, spears, shields, and a fierce look of wickedness in their eyes. But let's make no mistake, the giants you come up against every day can be just as imposing, just as intimidating, and just as wicked as Goliath. However, there is another—more important—similarity. Your giants are just as top-heavy and ready for defeat as Goliath was before David, if you face them in God's strength and power.

Let's name a few of those potential giants that call out to you like Goliath yelling at the Israelites, taunting you and claiming that you cannot fight back. They could include a fear of failure, a sense of inferiority, or a feeling that you are not qualified for the destiny you would like to pursue. How about the giants that many people face at some time in their lives: jealousy, anger, lust, pride, greed, or envy, to name just a few?

These enemies of your destiny don't always come out in the open and identify themselves. In fact, in some instances you may not even fully realize the power they exert. Often they are camouflaged as *attitudes* you have toward others: your tendency to shy away from situations that challenge you in certain ways; feelings of anxiety, anger, or any emotion that pushes you in a direction you don't want to go; or even words of unkindness or bitterness that slip off your tongue when you're being honest.

Whatever their camouflage, they are there, and if you take time to reflect on your life, and—most importantly—to ask God to uncover the issues that negatively impact your life, you will soon begin to identify the giants that can hold you back from your full destiny.

The Bible tells us that in our quest for God's best, our enemies often don't come out against us as flesh-and-blood foes. But they are nonetheless wicked and destructive—even more so, in fact, than if they had the look of a real-life giant like Goliath. You see, they are armed with the hatred and demonic destructive potential of the devil himself. The apostle Paul describes them as the *"rulers of the darkness of this age"* and *"spiritual hosts of wickedness in the heavenly places."*[3]

I know those terms sound imposing and intimidating, and many people shrink back in fear when they think of the devil and his demonic forces arrayed to do battle against them as *"principalities and powers."* But I have good news for you: you have no reason to fear the enemy, because in the name of Jesus he is a defeated foe, and if you are equipped with the battle gear God has provided for you to defeat him,

---

3. Ephesians 6:12.

the devil will run from you in terror because he will see Jesus, who fights your battles for you.

> YOU HAVE NO REASON TO FEAR THE ENEMY,
> BECAUSE IN THE NAME OF JESUS HE IS A DEFEATED FOE.

THE WEAPONS OF YOUR WARFARE

God declares in His Word that your weapons are not the kind that this world can forge. They're not metal or stone, nuclear or chemical. Instead, He tells us that they are filled with divine power that will enable you to demolish the attacks and strongholds that the enemy builds in an attempt to hold you back.

THE NAME OF JESUS

Your first and most important weapon—in fact, the most powerful resource against the devil and all his strategies against you—is the blood of Jesus. There is simply nothing stronger or more effective that you can wield to defeat the giants that come against you—whether spiritual dangers and foes, illness and physical attacks, or even the attacks from individuals. The devil and his minions are fearful of the blood of Jesus and what it stands for, and when you declare it verbally and with authority against the foes that come against you, they will flee.

I strongly encourage you to symbolically apply the blood of Jesus to all things that pertain to you, from your past, present, and future, to your destiny, your family, your relationships, your employment— quite literally, everything that needs to be protected from the wiles of the devil. I challenge you to use your voice and, on a daily basis, say something as simple as, "Jesus, I apply your blood to every area of my life. I apply your blood to every part of my past, to my present life, my responsibilities, opportunities, and obligations. And I apply the blood of Jesus to my future, to my destiny, to the things that you have planned for me. I apply the blood of Jesus over my family, my relationships, and everything else that pertains to me. I declare and believe that your blood, Jesus, covers, protects, and defends all that is part of my life."

> I DECLARE AND BELIEVE THAT YOUR BLOOD, JESUS, COVERS, PROTECTS, AND DEFENDS ALL THAT IS PART OF MY LIFE.

THE WORD OF GOD

The next most important weapon that you must wield against the enemy is the Word of God. You must battle the attacks and intimidation of the enemy—which are all built on lies—with the truth, and there is only one reservoir of absolute truth: the Word of God. Just before He suffered the cruelty of crucifixion and death for our sins, Jesus prayed for us, asking God to *"sanctify"* us—to set us apart as wholly dedicated to Him—through the truth, adding with emphasis, *"Your Word is truth."*[4]

There is simply no other foundation of truth than Scripture, and while the world may have some good systems for strengthening your mind and fortifying it with self-determination, confidence, and courage, in the end there is no substitute for the absolute Word of your heavenly Father. When he faced overwhelming situations,

4. John 17:17.

circumstances, and enemies, King David prayed that God would lead him to the *"rock that is higher than I."*[5]

The same goes for you. Day in and day out you are going to be barraged by the changes of life and by attacks of the enemy that will sometimes threaten to overtake you, and the only thing that is going to keep you consistent is the truth. When you are battling fear, worry, confusion, unbelief, apathy—all of them attacks that the enemy will use against you—you need a weapon with which to effectively battle. That weapon is the Word of God. God's Word is more powerful than the enemy's attacks, and more powerful than the most destructive accusations and negative words of your critics, because truth is stronger than lies.

Jesus said that in Him you will know the truth and the truth will set you free.[6] But friend, as I have often said, it is the truth you *know* that sets you free, not the truth you *don't* know. In His Word, God tells you who you are in Christ, what you can do, and how to live effectively in the liberty and authority He has given you through His Son. The more skillful you are in handling and using the Word in every situation, the more you will be able to defend yourself and your destiny, and the more able you will be to embrace all the promises God has made on your behalf.

Jesus is the perfect example of using the weapon of the Word! When Jesus faced the devil in the wilderness, He opposed his lies with the Word of God. In each case, when Jesus declared the truth, the enemy was defeated. Similarly, when you declare God's Word into any situation or circumstance you face, it cuts away the lies and confusion with the clarity of God's truth. David said that God's Word was a *"lamp"* to his feet, and a *"light"* to his path, and so it is with you.[7] The Word illuminates your spiritual surroundings, penetrates

---

5. Psalm 61:2.
6. See John 8:32.
7. Psalm 119:105.

the darkness with the radiance of His holiness, goodness, and mercy, and gives you absolute direction for your life.

To build on what we saw in chapter 6, this is why it is so crucial for you to spend time reading, studying, meditating on, and intimately knowing the Word of God, so that when the enemy comes, you can raise the standard of truth against him. The Word of God is, in reality, a sword—the *"sword of the Spirit,"* as the apostle Paul calls it.[8] And friend, just as it was with Jesus, with Paul, and with all the most effective and fruitful saints down through the ages, the Word of God is the most powerful weapon you can wield in all the battles you face. The more you give yourself to it, the more you pour His Word into your heart, mind, and spirit, the more you will be prepared, at a moment's notice, to wield it boldly and with authority against the attacks of the enemy.

STAND IN FAITH

The Word of God will prepare you to use another crucial piece of your spiritual armor, what the apostle Paul calls the *"shield of faith."*[9] As I have said elsewhere in this book, faith is key to advancing in your quest for God's best. The Bible says that without faith, you cannot even please God, and it is certain that without it you cannot embrace the things that He has for us.[10] As they spent time with Jesus and watched Him at work healing the sick, raising the dead, and ministering to those around Him, Jesus' disciples began to understand that they would not be able to do what they saw Him do or match His authority, compassion, and power without the crucial element of faith. That is why they asked Jesus one day, *"Increase our faith."*[11] Jesus' simple but profound response to their request was to tell them that the *quantity* of their faith wasn't the key, but the *quality*. Pointing to a nearby tree He said, *"If you have faith as small as a mustard seed, you*

8. Ephesians 6:17.
9. Ephesians 6:16.
10. See Hebrews 11:6.
11. Luke 17:5.

can say to this mulberry tree, 'Be uprooted and planted in the sea,' and it will obey you."[12]

What Jesus meant is that with just a little faith in God you can do miracles—in fact, greater miracles than He did when He walked the earth, because He is sitting at the right hand of the Father on your behalf.[13]

But just as important to your destiny, this very same faith also acts as a shield to protect you from all the "fiery arrows" that the enemy will shoot at you on a daily basis—arrows of doubt, fear, unbelief, sickness, poverty, and the like. *Without* this shield of faith you are going to be vulnerable to the attacks that will most certainly come against you each and every day. Your confidence in God will suffer, and you will find confusion and fear coming over you like storm clouds. But *with* that shield firmly in front of you, you can and will move boldly ahead with all the authority of Christ, defeating the devil and all the giants he places in your way, and taking your destiny—God's Promised Land for you—with confidence. Yes, the attacks will still come, and the enemy will continue to try to derail you. But with faith you will not be deterred!

So how do you access the faith you need to stand? Like many others, maybe you struggle with believing God, and perhaps doubt, fear, and unbelief assail you on a regular basis. But I am here to declare to you that God does not condemn you. Instead He has provided the simple resource to fill you with all the faith you need. The apostle Paul confirms that faith will come to you through God's Word.[14]

Yes, it's that simple. There is no complicated process for getting faith. It will come to each person regardless of their standing in this world, simply by saturating their mind with the truth of Scripture. And while it only takes a *"mustard seed"* of faith to move a mountain,[15]

---

12. Luke 17:6 NIV.
13. See John 14:12.
14. See Romans 10:17.
15. Luke 17:6.

the more you give yourself to know God through His Word, the stronger your faith will become, and the more boldly you can move into the destiny God has planned for you.

> THE MORE YOU GIVE YOURSELF TO KNOW GOD THROUGH HIS WORD, THE STRONGER YOUR FAITH WILL BECOME.

HAVING DONE ALL—STAND!

Friend, you are a fighter—and a winner! I believe that strongly about you, because I know that God is on your side. You were created to know and love Him, and to walk in the full destiny He has created for you. But just like His people down through history, you must stand and fight the enemy armed with the weapons and armor that God has given you—the blood of Jesus, the truth of His Word, and faith.

However, there is one thing that you must remember as you stand and fight the enemy: ultimately, the battle is not yours, but the Lord's. Yes, God calls you to prepare, to stand with the blood of Jesus applied to your life and circumstances, to stand with the Word of God as a sword in your hand, and to stand with the shield of faith covering you. But having done all, in the end you must rely on Him to win your battles. It sounds like a contradiction, but while you actively stand and fight the enemy, at the same time God wants you to "stand still" and see the victory He will work on your behalf.

You don't have to be strong in your own strength. Instead, you are to be *"strong in the Lord and in the power of His might."*[16] In fact, God

---

16. Ephesians 6:10.

is most able to work in and through you when you are at your weakest, because it is at that point, when you have no ability and power in yourself, that you throw yourself entirely on God and His provision. In those moments His miracle power can be most evident in your circumstances.

In the next chapter we will explore this powerful connection between your weakness and God's strength.

**WHEN YOU STEP FORWARD,
GOD IS STILL ALWAYS ONE STEP AHEAD.**

FAVOR
TAKEAWAY

9

STRENGTH THROUGH WEAKNESS

I heard a story not long ago about a young man who lost his left arm in an accident, and decided to take up judo as a part of his rehabilitation. His teacher was an aged Japanese judo master—called a *sensei*—and within just a few weeks the young man had progressed far beyond his own expectations. However, he was puzzled because as well as he was doing, the old master had taught him only one judo move. "Sensei," the young man protested one day. "Shouldn't I be learning some more moves like the other students?" The old man looked at him for a moment before responding. "You will never need any more moves than the one I have taught you," he replied evenly

A few months later the *sensei* took the young man to his first judo tournament, where, although he had only one arm, the young man easily won his first two matches. The next match was more difficult, but again, in just a round or two, the young man used the one move he knew to outmaneuver his skilled opponent—and was again victorious.

Amazingly, the handicapped young man made it all the way to the championship match, where his opponent was stronger and more skilled than anyone he had faced before. The young man looked to be seriously overmatched! The unfairness was so apparent that the referee stepped in to stop the match when the *sensei* called out, "Let them continue!"

As the match progressed the two sparred until the young man's opponent became careless and let down his guard—giving the young man the opportunity he needed to use his one move to pin his challenger and win the championship.

Afterward the *sensei* explained to the young man what it was that had brought him victory. "The move I taught you is one of the most difficult in judo," said the *sensei*, "and you mastered it because it is the only tool you had. But there is something else. The only way your opponent could have defended against this move was to grab your left arm. You see, your weakness in the ring became your strength."

WE ALL HAVE WEAKNESSES

We have all seen, and maybe even know, individuals whose lives have been drastically altered through a terrible accident or injury that closes the door on a once-hoped-for future. A few weeks ago I watched a football game in which a talented player was on the receiving end of a vicious tackle that ended his season—and very possibly his career. Likewise, over the past several years we have seen many strong, hopeful young men and women go off to war in the Middle East, only to come home permanently disabled and with their futures violently changed. Where there was once strength and confidence, weakness and uncertainty now reign.

For others, the limitations are the result of internal traumas that have taken a devastating toll. Physical or emotional abuse suffered as children has impacted many, severely hampering their hopes and dreams. Others are dealing with the turmoil of broken relationships, divorce, or the unexpected death of a loved one. The joyful anticipation they had for the future with the one they loved has been replaced by sorrow, guilt, shame, and a myriad of other emotions.

Most often, however, it seems to be our past with its sin, mistakes, and missteps, along with present-day habits, addictions, and personal issues, that try to hold us back, clawing at us with condemnation and accusation, defying us to move ahead into the Promised Land of our God-given futures. Friend, it is at this point—when we are at our weakest and most vulnerable—that God loves to come in with His strength, blowing away obstacles and lifting us up to the mountaintop of His miraculous power.

> WHEN WE ARE AT OUR WEAKEST AND MOST VULNERABLE, GOD LOVES TO COME IN WITH HIS STRENGTH, BLOWING AWAY OBSTACLES AND LIFTING US UP TO THE MOUNTAINTOP OF HIS MIRACULOUS POWER.

GOD WORKS IN AND THROUGH OUR WEAKNESS

It's no secret that we live in a world that glorifies self-confidence, strength, and self-determination while shunning personal weakness and limitations. No one wants to look dependent, clumsy, awkward, or needy. Thumb through a pile of resumés and you'll find that invariably they are packed with examples of people's accomplishments, strengths, talents, and abilities. Rarely will one ever admit to being weak or uncertain in an area where strength and confidence are required—even though we all know no one is perfect.

It is interesting, then, to discover that nearly every person in Scripture whom God used mightily was seriously flawed, weak, and unconfident in the purpose to which God had called them. Just consider:

+ Moses, whom God placed before Pharaoh to be a spokesman for His people Israel, was *"slow of speech"*—that is, he had a stutter.[1]

+ Abraham and Sarah were well beyond child-bearing years when God gave them a son, Isaac, thus beginning the fulfillment of the promise that He would make Abraham's offspring more than the sand of the sea. They were senior citizens before they had their first child![2]

+ Gideon was so terrified of the enemies of Israel that he worked his fields in the middle of the night to keep them from stealing from him. Yet God called him a *"mighty man of valor,"* and commissioned him in his weakness and timidity to lead the children of Israel to victory over their oppressors.[3]

+ David was the youngest of Jesse's sons, a lowly shepherd boy all but forgotten in the wilderness, yet God called him to lead Israel, and loved him as a *"man after My own heart."*[4]

+ Peter denied Jesus, but God raised him up to be a key leader of the early church.

+ Saul terrorized the early church, even cheering as one of its beloved leaders, Stephen, was stoned for his faith in Christ.[5] Yet God raised Saul up to become the apostle Paul.

And the stories of weakness to greatness are not just found in the Bible! I've always been intrigued by how successful people came into their realm of influence, and often have discovered that some of the

---

1. Exodus 4:10.
2. See Hebrews 11:12.
3. See Judges 6:12.
4. Acts 13:22.
5. See Acts 22:20.

individuals considered the greatest in their fields were once considered failures.

+ Michael Jordan, thought by many to be the greatest basketball player of all time, was cut from his high school basketball team. He once noted that he had missed more than 9,000 shots in his career, lost nearly 300 games, and on more than two dozen occasions was expected to make a game-winning shot—and missed. "I have failed over and over and over again in my life," he reflected. "And that is why I succeed."

+ After just one performance Elvis Presley was fired by the manager of the Grand Ole Opry with the advice, "You ain't going nowhere, son. You ought to go back to driving a truck."

+ When they were just starting out, the Beatles were told by a record company they approached that their sound wasn't right, and, besides, "guitar music is on its way out."

+ Oprah Winfrey was once fired from a job as a news reporter because she was "unfit for TV."

+ As a young man Walt Disney was fired by a newspaper editor who had hired him as an artist, because he apparently lacked imagination and had no good ideas.

+ Albert Einstein's teachers thought he might be mentally handicapped because he did not speak until he was four and couldn't read until he was seven.

+ Before her iconic *I Love Lucy* went down in history as the greatest comedy show of all time, Lucille Ball was considered little more than a B movie star with no future. Even her drama instructor suggested that she find another line of work.[6]

---

6. Bud Bilanich, "50 Famous People," BudBilanich.com, http://www.budbilanich.com/50-famous-people-who-failed-at-their-first-attempt-at-career-success (accessed March 3, 2017).

As you can see, if these folks had listened to others, or been influenced by their own perceived weaknesses and lack, they would have missed their historic destinies, and the world would have been a little poorer because of it.

How about you? Has someone spoken a negative word over your dream, or has your own sense of inadequacy prevented you from stepping out into the destiny God has for you? Have you been told you're "too stupid" to succeed, as a teacher once told Thomas Edison? Don't forget he's the one who invented the first commercially successful light bulb, the phonograph, motion pictures, and other innovations we now take for granted. Maybe you've had a tough time succeeding in school, as did the great twentieth-century statesman Sir Winston Churchill, who flunked sixth grade. Or perhaps you have faced issues with anxiety or depression, as did Abraham Lincoln, who suffered a nervous breakdown years before becoming president of the United States.

My point here is that despite what others have said, the negative things you may have believed about yourself, or even actual limitations you may suffer, you can still reach your destiny, just as countless individuals before you have. And with God on your side, and His Word as your guide, the simple truth is that you can't lose, because He delights to do His will through those who are convinced of their own inadequacy.

WITH GOD ON YOUR SIDE, AND HIS WORD AS YOUR GUIDE, THE SIMPLE TRUTH IS THAT YOU CAN'T LOSE.

YOU'RE STRONGEST AT YOUR WEAKEST

Think about your own weaknesses, the place in your life where you feel the most vulnerable, insignificant, imperfect, or lacking, or where, in your own mind, the word "failure" has been imprinted in bold letters. It is quite likely that God will use that place of failure and fault as a place of destiny and strength in your life.

The awesome thing about the heart of God—the place where our destinies are designed and forged—is that it is filled with mercy, grace, and help for the weak. The very place where you are weakest—in your abilities, in your past sins and mistakes, and in your present-day struggles—is where God delights to fill you with His strength.

The apostle Paul discovered this when he asked God to help him in a particular weakness he had. Now, Scripture does not make it clear just what that weakness was, but we are told that, because Paul had been given such an abundance of authority and revelation in the things of God, he also was afflicted with a *"thorn in the flesh"* to keep him humble and grounded. This thorn, or weakness, was obviously something that Paul wanted to be delivered from very much, because he tells us in 2 Corinthians 12 that he sought the Lord diligently on three separate occasions to have it taken away from him.

But God had something else in mind. "My grace is the only thing you need," God in effect told Paul, "because my strength and power are made perfect when you are weak."[7] God was telling this strong leader, the great apostle Paul, who withstood many conflicts and enemies throughout his life and who had spent much of his life being self-adequate and capable, that he was most useful to God when he was at his *weakest*.

YOUR WAY OR GOD'S WAY?

What went for Paul goes for each of us as well. We are all prone to pride, to rely on our own strength and abilities, and to shun or

7. See 2 Corinthians 12:9.

deny our limitations and weaknesses. But guess what? Each of us has those limitations in our lives, different for each person, but no less evident—and no less of a "thorn" than they were to the great apostle. And just as they did for Paul, those limitations and weaknesses force us to run to the Lord for His grace, mercy, and strength as we pursue His best for our lives.

The Bible is clear that the one thing God hates more than almost anything else in people is pride. In fact, we are told that God resists a person who is proud, arrogant, and committed to his or her own merits rather than God's grace. By contrast, we are told that He gives unlimited grace and help to the humble, to those who are convinced of their own weakness and inability to succeed on their own.[8]

FAITH OF A CHILD

Jesus emphasized that a prerequisite to success and fruitfulness in God's kingdom is a childlike faith and dependence upon God. I recall a story I heard about a man on a hike one afternoon in the forest with his young eight-year-old son. The man had planned on just a half-hour stroll on a well-traveled path through the woods to see if he and his boy might spot a deer, fox, or some other wildlife.

But the path that they were on, unfamiliar to the father, turned into a winding, confusing maze of many intersecting paths. Worse yet, the afternoon sun that had brightened their day had fallen into a gathering dusk, and the paths started to become hard to distinguish. Before long, father and son were thoroughly lost. While he kept up a cheerful banter with his trusting son, inside the father was beginning to panic as he tried to lead them back the way they had come. As the sun went down and dusk changed to darkness, the father sped up his pace in a frantic attempt to make it back to the main road where their car was parked. He could feel his son's hand tighten in his own, and looking down he noticed that his son's smile had turned into an

---

8. See, for example, Psalm 138:6; Proverbs 3:34; 29:3; Matthew 23:12; and James 4:6.

expression of concern as he looked up into his father's eyes. His son didn't say a word but held tightly to his father's hand and followed him step for step.

Finally, as the two were stumbling along in nearly pitch-dark night, the father heard the sound of automobiles and the faint glow of their headlights, and in a few more moments the two stepped out onto the highway, just yards from where the father had parked their car. Later, as they were driving home, the father praised his boy for staying brave and not crying, even when it seemed they might be seriously lost. "Dad, I knew that as long as I hung on to your hand I'd be okay," the lad responded. "I knew you'd find the way."

Friend, *that* is precisely the kind of faith God wants you to have in His leadership in your life. If you are like most people, the road you have traveled in life has included a fair share of twists and turns you did not plan on taking. And it is probable that, as you forge ahead to God's unfolding destiny in your life, you will face many more uncertain paths and dark roads that will tempt you to be fearful for your future. But just like the son who held tightly to his father's hand, as you hold tenaciously to the Lord, following along in the direction He leads, you will make it to the light of His plan for you—every time.

A child knows his weakness and limitations, and while he may test his wings and act courageous in the comfort of familiar surroundings, in times of perceived danger and uncertainty he is eager for mom or dad to be there to protect him and lead the way. Each of us must relate to God in the same way, letting go of our own strength and wisdom—which are always insufficient to fulfill God's plan—and quietly, confidently relying on His perfect wisdom and direction for us.

NO SHAME IN WEAKNESS

While the world shuns weakness and glorifies strength, in God's kingdom it is just the opposite. There can be only one strong One, almighty God, and there can be only one source for the strength we need—in His presence.

> WHILE THE WORLD SHUNS WEAKNESS AND GLORIFIES STRENGTH, IN GOD'S KINGDOM IT IS JUST THE OPPOSITE.

There is no shame in that. In fact, God waits patiently for each of us to come to the end of our own strength and abilities, to acknowledge our weakness, and to actively place our trust in Him alone. It is at that point that He will most actively step into our circumstances and become the answer to our deepest needs—whatever those needs are. Doors that we could not pry open on our own swing wide when we step aside and let Him be the answer. Life's puzzles that caused us heartache or apprehension fall into place when we cease trying to solve them on our own. Obstacles to relationships that were impossible to reconcile because of bitterness, unforgiveness, and pride suddenly melt away as we take our hands off and ask God for His strength to become perfect in our weakness.

I personally know of individuals who were accepted to schools, hired for jobs, and given professional positions that were beyond their ability simply because they actively placed their destinies into God's hands and asked Him to open doors. I have seen marriages healed and parents reconciled to lost children when God was invited to be Lord of the situation.

It is also at this place of acknowledged weakness that true greatness is forged. Did you know that the most priceless diamonds in the world looked like nothing more than plain and unattractive stones before being sculpted by a master diamond cutter? Similarly, a fine musical instrument, like a Stradivarius violin, is nothing more than wood and wire strings until it is taken up by a master, in whose delicate and skillful hands it becomes priceless. Friend, underneath all your weakness, imperfections, and lack is a masterpiece that God is just waiting to bring out into perfection.

WILLING TO WAIT

And there is one main thing you can do to help Him make that happen: you can wait. That's right. Our human mind thinks that improving, becoming, and progressing takes effort on our part—that it takes pushing and striving to make something happen. But in God's economy that is not the case. All God wants you to do is wait for Him. Sculptor Gutson Borglum, famous for carving the visages of four American presidents—George Washington, Thomas Jefferson, Abraham Lincoln, and Theodore Roosevelt—into the granite rock of Mount Rushmore, South Dakota, was once asked how he was able to create such accurate likenesses of the four historic figures. He responded that the four stone figures had been waiting there from the time the earth began. "All I had to do was dynamite 400,000 tons of granite to bring them into view," he explained. If you look at the base of Mount Rushmore, you will see those 400,000 tons of granite that were blown, hammered, and chipped away to reveal those historic faces. It's a mass of rubble that few see, above which are the noble and breathtaking masterpiece sculptures that were revealed when that rubble was hammered away.

In the same way, your God-designed character, destiny, and future are all there, deep inside of you, just as He created them. Yes, there may be a lot of "rock" and rubble to be chipped away so that the perfection of what He created will come forth. That is His job as the Master Sculptor, and, like the perfectly sculpted statues beneath the rock of Mount Rushmore, you have no strength or ability to help Him complete the work to get you there. All you can do is wait and let Him do what needs to be done.

The prophet Isaiah tells us that those who *"wait on the* Lord*"* will be renewed in strength. They will *"mount up with wings like eagles."*[9] Have you ever seen an eagle as she flies effortlessly and majestically above all our earth-bound troubles and burdens? The analogy is so perfect for how God empowers those of us who need His strength. Under His powerful guidance you will not grow weary in the pursuit of what He has called you to do and be, and you will never faint through being fearful or over-burdened.

Yes, you will be challenged, and yes, your faith will be stretched. That is all a part of growing in maturity and being seasoned as a true son or daughter of God. But Jesus assures us that the burden He calls us to bear in our quest for God's best will be light.[10] Our life can be an unbroken walk of deep joy and abiding peace even during the wilderness seasons to which He calls each of us in His perfect plan in order to conform and "sculpt" us to that masterpiece that is in His mind's eye—if we only keep our gaze on Him. That is His promise.

---

9. Isaiah 40:31.
10. See Matthew 11:30.

BOUNDLESS STRENGTH IS REALLY
LIMITLESS RELIANCE ON GOD.

FAVOR
TAKEAWAY

10

FACING ADVERSITY VICTORIOUSLY

It is considered one of the most memorable performances in Olympic history, and yet, amazingly, few witnessed the courage and determination with which John Stephen Akhwari concluded the marathon at the 1968 Mexico City Olympic Games. A world-class long distance runner, Akhwari was naturally chosen to represent his native Tanzania in the Olympic marathon, the grueling 26.2-mile race that would take runners through a variety of terrains in Mexico City before bringing them back to finish before a cheering crowd in the massive Olympic stadium.

While Akhwari had trained diligently for the honor of representing his country, he was not prepared for running in the high altitude of Mexico City, and before long his legs cramped badly. Nonetheless, he held his own through much of the first half of the contest, until, as other competitors were jockeying for position, Akhwari was bumped, fell to the ground, and severely injured his leg and shoulder. As the rest of the runners quickly sped ahead, Akhwari slowly got up, and although in pain and barely able to continue, hobbled on along the race route.

Sometimes jogging, sometimes walking, and at times stopping to rest and deal with the pain he was in, Akhwari finally struggled into the Olympic stadium, over an hour after the other fifty-six runners had finished—completely alone but driven by a determination to not quit until he had completed the assignment with which he had been commissioned by his nation.

Stadium nearly empty—it was the last running event of the Olympic Games—John Stephen Akhwari finally crossed the finish line and took his well-deserved place in Olympic history. Asked later why he persevered through the pain and personal humiliation of being the last lonely runner in a race where he had hoped to attain glory for himself and his people, Akhwari responded with the words that have inspired millions ever since.

"My country did not send me 11,000 kilometers to start the Olympic marathon," Akhwari told a news reporter. "They sent me here to finish it."[1]

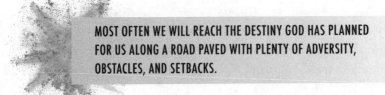

MOST OFTEN WE WILL REACH THE DESTINY GOD HAS PLANNED FOR US ALONG A ROAD PAVED WITH PLENTY OF ADVERSITY, OBSTACLES, AND SETBACKS.

CREATED AND COMMISSIONED FOR SUCCESS

In a culture that worships the slick, media-embellished version of success—with trophies, ticker-tape acclaim, and larger-than-life images—it can be difficult to face the truth that real life usually looks far different, that most often we will reach the destiny God has planned

---

1. John Stephen Akhwari, quoted in "Strange but True," *Runner's World*, July 6, 2012, http://www.runnersworld.com/olympics/strange-but-true (accessed March 3, 2017).

for us along by taking a road paved with plenty of adversity, obstacles, and setbacks.

But remember that just as John Stephen Akhwari's country didn't send him to the Olympics with the expectation that he would give up under adversity, in the same way God didn't create and commission you to give up halfway toward the glorious destiny He has determined for you. He created you for success and victory, and it will come! Your job is to keep your eyes on Him and your heart and efforts focused on the dreams He has placed within your heart.

When Akhwari climbed aboard the plane that took him back to his home in Tanzania after the Olympic Games, I am sure he was deeply disappointed that he had not been able to do better on behalf of his country. And few people—even in his homeland—would have blamed him had he chosen to quit after he fell rather than struggle on in pain over twelve more miles to the solitary completion of his task.

While he never came close to winning an Olympic medal, his determination to finish what he had started, to do all he could on behalf of his country and his people, led to rewards I am sure Akhwari has valued throughout his life far more than he would an Olympic gold medal. You see, when he returned to Tanzania, waiting for him was a nation and people who considered him a hero. A few years after the Olympic Games, his government awarded him its National Hero Medal of Honor for his actions, and he has served as a goodwill ambassador for several Olympic Games since, encouraging many people to persevere in the face of difficulties and hardships.

"WELL DONE"

The apostle Paul was a man who knew plenty of hardship and adversity in the pursuit of his destiny. He had given up a lot, in human terms, to follow Christ. A well-educated man with the respect of the religious leaders, Paul left behind all that had meant so much to him when Jesus met him dramatically on the road to Damascus. He turned his heart to following hard after God and received the reward of a lifetime of fruitfulness in God's kingdom.

In fact, when weighed against the incomparable riches that his destiny in Christ offered, Paul referred to his old life—the dreams, the successes, and all the trappings of worldly achievement—as *"rubbish,"* saying that everything that had once seemed so important to him he counted as loss, compared to finding his destiny in Christ.[2]

And what did that destiny look like? Well, for sure it included much fruitfulness as he traveled across the then-known world, preaching the gospel, establishing churches, and encouraging believers in their faith in Christ. He made many beloved friends, had the opportunity to see many new places, and gained distinction as one of the premier leaders of the New Testament church. Yes, many people respected and esteemed him.

But all the success and rich fulfillment came with a price. For starters, the Jewish religious officials of his former life placed a price on his head, and Paul spent much of the rest of his life a hunted man. He was sometimes ridiculed by the very people to whom he ministered, as he laid down his life for the gospel. He was persecuted and beaten for the sake of his faith and his destiny in Christ.

In 2 Corinthians 11 this esteemed apostle listed some of the adversities he faced in his journey to fulfill the call that God had placed on him. From shipwrecks, beatings, nakedness, and facing whatever weather that came along, to untold dangers and, ultimately, prison in Rome where he at last gave up his life because of the destiny to which God had called him—Paul counted it all as of no account, just circumstances he was called upon to face as he fulfilled his God-given destiny.

And at the end of that road, when he knew his days were numbered and that he would shortly face the Roman executioner, the apostle Paul had this to say: *"I have fought the good fight, I have finished*

---

2. Philippians 3:7–8.

the race, I have kept the faith. Finally, there is laid up for me the crown of righteousness, which the Lord, the righteous Judge, will give to me on that Day...."[3]

You see, like the faithful and single-minded Olympic marathon runner, the apostle Paul had kept his eyes on the real prize, the commendation and approval of the One who had commissioned him. As a trained and well-connected Jewish man, Paul could have had plenty of worldly acclaim and all that goes with it. But long ago he had settled what he really wanted out of life, and with singleness of heart and mind he went after it. His sole desire was to one day stand before His Lord and hear Him say: "Well done, good and faithful servant."

THE ADVERSITIES OF LIFE

Friend, just like John Stephen Akhwari, and just like the apostle Paul, you are in a race. Yes, your contest most likely looks far different than Akhwari's or Paul's. You're not in a physical race representing your nation on the world's biggest athletic stage, hurting from head to toe. And you probably aren't facing shipwrecks, beatings, and other grave dangers like the great apostle. But Scripture nonetheless likens your walk of faith to a race, filled with obstacles and pitfalls that can hurt and hold you back. The adversities you face as you daily pursue your passions and dreams are no less real and no less painful than the ones that attacked the runner and the apostle, and they will require the same determination and resolve that these men embraced for you to overcome them and make it all the way to victory.

Perhaps you are a single mom or dad juggling parenting, school, job, and all the other responsibilities of life, while trying to keep your eyes on the goal of career, ministry, or other destiny that God has placed in your heart. You have walked the walk of faith for so long, while the bright spots of hope and success seemed few and far between. You wonder if you can go on much longer without a breakthrough.

---

3. 2 Timothy 4:7–8.

You are beginning to think that the race may be too long, the obstacles and adversities too severe for you to make it all the way to your goal.

Or maybe you're a man or woman trying to make ends meet for your family in an economy that seems to less and less value hard-working and dependable individuals with integrity and motivation. You have stuck it out in a job that is far beneath your abilities and goals, or had a door slammed on you one too many times as you have patiently sought a place where you can grow while providing well for the ones you love. You're wondering if such a place exists for everyone but you, and you have had fleeting thoughts of just throwing in the towel and giving up.

Similarly, I wonder how many college students are out there who began their race with excitement, hope, and anticipation of finishing their education and moving into a profession that would give them a place of purpose and godly influence. But financial obstacles, academic hardship, or even a failure or two in some aspect of their chosen course of study have left them reeling and unsure of their future.

"Did I miss God's best?" they wonder. "Did I blow it? Should I have studied harder? Maybe I'm just not cut out for college?" Where confidence and faith once reigned, apprehension, confusion, and uncertainty now whirl about like a storm.

I know, also, that there are men and women reading these pages who are convinced that whatever opportunities they once had in life have been destroyed through missteps, mistakes, sins, and lifestyles that placed obstacles in the path of their destiny—obstacles that now seem like immoveable boulders. While faith and a clear vision of God's direction once guided them, the haze of regret and remorse over poor choices now has them groping for light and assurance of tomorrow.

Life has a way of throwing curveballs at us that can threaten to turn us aside from our God-given destiny. Often those hardships are the result of circumstances beyond our control. Sickness, an accident, the loss of a job, the responses of others, or a situation that we just didn't see coming can change life and make our road rough and rocky. In other instances our own foolishness, sin, or mistakes can bring us into a place of hardship and adversity. But despite the source of adversity in our lives, our God is master over all of it, and nothing we face takes Him by surprise. Moreover, it is His delight to bring us victory in the very face of our hardships—regardless of their cause. And, despite how problems and adversity may set us back, God is never at a loss.

Friend, in my own life, no matter how tough or impossible a situation has seemed, I have never heard God respond with, "Wow! I didn't see that coming! That may be more than Henry and I can deal with." God is *always* bigger than anything we face, and our posture of insistent faith in Him will ensure victory.

As we were establishing our church and ministry in Fort Lauderdale, Faith Center Ministries, we faced our share of obstacles that tried our faith to an incredible degree. And there were times when we were actually tempted to doubt the future of the work that God had placed in our hands. But through it all, as we kept our hearts and minds focused on God and His truth, He assured us that He was in control and that we would see victory as we persevered on the course He set for us.

GOD IS ALWAYS BIGGER THAN ANYTHING WE FACE, AND OUR POSTURE OF INSISTENT FAITH IN HIM WILL ENSURE VICTORY.

DESTINED TO WIN

Friend, the truth is that before you were born, God had already spoken destiny and success over your life, and now that you are well on the road to His destiny for you, God is committed more than ever to your success. You are destined to win the race He has set before you. And even though you face adversities, they have no power to derail you and can, in fact, serve to make you stronger and more determined as you reach for greatness.

The key to your victory over obstacles and adversity—stated many times in Scripture—is endurance, refusing to let go of God's promise to complete His work in you and to bring you to your destiny. Those who persevere in the face of adversity will win. The key is simply to not give up. The writer of the book of Hebrews tells us that countless individuals down through history have been where we stand today, facing the same hardships, obstacles, and adversities that you and I face in our lives. "Lay aside every weight and distraction that the enemy uses to try to lead you off the path of God's perfect plan for you," we are counseled, "and run with endurance and patience the race that is before you, keeping your eyes fixed on Jesus, the author and completer of your faith."[4]

That means letting go of every past defeat, failure, fault, and sin, plunging it all under the blood of Jesus. Everything the enemy tries to use to keep you from the full destiny God has offered you, you must reject!

While I can assure you that God has great things for you in the here and now—prosperity, success, and unfettered joy for you and your family—the ultimate goal, the prize that you are reaching for, is Jesus. The goal is to know Him, love Him, and be conformed to the image of His glory. That is your true destiny. Every other success and attainment in life, regardless of how glorious, will one day pale to being found complete in Him.

---

4. See Hebrews 12:1–2.

Just like John Stephen Akhwari, whose victory came not in winning a gold medal but in completing the race for his nation, when your days on earth are over, your reward and victory will come in having overcome every obstacle and adversity placed before you, completed the destiny for which God created you, and being able to declare with the apostle Paul: *"I have fought the good fight, I have finished the race, I have kept the faith. Finally, there is laid up for me the crown of righteousness...."*[5]

Friend, keep your eyes on the prize, and never stop asking and expecting God to do great things in your life. You were created for His best—for the here and now, and for all eternity. Believe it and receive it!

---

5. 2 Timothy 4:7–8.

YOU ARE IN A RACE
THAT YOU HAVE ALREADY WON.

FAVOR
TAKEAWAY

11

WHO'S DEFINING YOUR DESTINY?

If there is one thing I know from my years of pursuing God's best for my life, it is this: there will always be people who will try to persuade you to accept second best. Often it is those people you expected to *encourage* you in your quest for God's best. It's not too difficult to see why. If you reach out for God's best and succeed, there is a subtle reflection that they, perhaps, have let their own opportunities slip away. It is much easier for them to try to hold you back than to face head-on a need for change in their own lives.

Their words can hurt, and even cause you to question the wisdom of reaching and working and trusting God for more of what His Word promises. "You must think you're something special to be aiming that high," a friend or loved one might say to you when you share the dream God has placed in your heart.

Or, "Do you really believe that you're going to be accepted into that school? No one else in your family ever went to college. What makes you think you're any different?"

Or how about: "You don't have the skills or background for that career! You're setting your sights too high. Why don't you lower your expectations a notch or two?"

Or, "You're no preacher, teacher, or anything else like that. You're just plain folk like the rest of us. Get your head out of the clouds!"

How many parents have unwittingly held back a child from greatness simply because they thought that their son or daughter had ambitions that were too lofty? How many great doctors, engineers, educators, artists, or preachers has the world been denied because of the well-meaning counsel of a parent? "Son, I just don't want you to be disappointed when you realize that this course you've chosen is more than you can handle." Or, "Daughter, don't let that dream of being a professional musician steer you away from something more practical."

THE BATTLE OF CIRCUMSTANCE

But it's not just people who will make you want to give up. Circumstances and situations will also stare down your destiny and try to convince you that the price is too steep, that you are on the wrong track, or that you're in way over your head. A hefty bill you hadn't planned for, an illness that sets you back in your plans, an accident that lays you up, a pink slip from your job, or a pass-over on a promotion—there is no end to the circumstances that can appear out of nowhere to attack you at the core of your hope and threaten to shoot down your dream. If you are not vigilant in protecting your dream, before you know it you can become convinced that your expectations really are too high, and that you need to come back to the reality of a lesser blessing.

But friend, I am here to assure you that you didn't get it wrong and you haven't aimed too high. God has placed hopes, dreams, and a destiny in your heart, and it is important for you to guard them jealously and allow no one and nothing to talk you out of God's best. You must get it down deep into your spirit that God did not create you for mediocrity, for second best, or for a hand-me-down blessing. He created and commissioned you to receive and embrace the best He has to give.

You must never allow the naysayers, the obstacles, circumstances, or life's ups and downs to define your destiny. That is something for only you and God to determine, and His Word is clear that He has already got a solid handle on the direction He has for you. One of my favorite Scriptures—one I have shared with thousands of individuals as I have counseled them on their future—is Jeremiah 29:11, which makes it clear that God has a plan for each of our lives, a plan that is peaceful, prosperous, and filled with hope.

If that is the case, why is it that so many of God's people live in such a different realm, where doubts, anxiety, and uncertainty are constantly impeding their progress? I am convinced it is because God has designed our lives and structured our destinies in such a way that we must stay in agreement with Him and His Word in order to fulfill the plans He has for each of us. If we don't, if we allow opposing viewpoints and opinions to compete with the truth of God's Word for pre-eminence in their lives, we will spend our days in the kind of compromise to the world that would not even be a consideration if we turned our hearts completely to follow God and His Word.

Understand that God will not share His glory with anyone or anything. When you allow something other than God's truth to crowd into your thinking, and when you entertain doubts and allow unbelief to have even a small opening into your mind, the result is a conflict that will continue to assault your future until you make the choice to cast down those thoughts and opinions that oppose the truth and the realization of your destiny.

YOU CANNOT SERVE TWO MASTERS

Jesus said that you cannot serve two masters. It is a spiritual impossibility. You will either hold to Him and His promise for your life, or you will cave in to the compromise of this world.[1] God's plan for your life is predicated on your willingness to trust, obey, and follow Him with a devotion that allows no encumbrances and no competition. Where there is division in your mind or heart as to God's direction for your life, it is imperative that you surrender your plans, desires, and will to His. The writer of Proverbs emphasizes the importance of trusting in the Lord: *"Trust in the LORD with all your heart, and lean not on your own understanding; in all your ways acknowledge Him, and He shall direct your paths,"* the writer assures us.[2]

> GOD'S PLAN FOR YOUR LIFE IS PREDICATED ON YOUR WILLINGNESS TO TRUST, OBEY, AND FOLLOW HIM WITH A DEVOTION THAT ALLOWS NO ENCUMBRANCES AND NO COMPETITION.

The apostle James makes it clear that instability in your determination to follow the Lord and trust His direction is a huge obstacle to your destiny. He compares the person who wavers in his or her faith in God to a wave that is driven and tossed. *"Let not that man suppose that He will receive anything from the Lord."*[3] You see, even though the Lord loves you and is committed to your good, if you are walking on two sides of the road—trying to trust God while still listening to the world's advice and counsel—He will starve you out until, in desperation, you turn fully and completely to Him.

Reaching your full potential—conformity to the image of Christ and walking in the full blessing He has purchased for you—is too wonderful a reality for Him to allow anything less in your life.

---

1. See Luke 16:13.
2. Proverbs 3:5–6.
3. James 1:7.

THE EXAMPLE OF ISRAEL

The children of Israel provide one of the starkest examples of a people who could not decide who to follow: God or the nations around them. They certainly had faced plenty of instances where God had led them even in their rebellion, loving them and patiently guiding them into the green pastures of His perfect will for them. But for some reason, throughout biblical history they never seemed to learn that God's ways were far more wise and good than the counsel of those around them.

In 1 Kings we are introduced to Ahab, one of the many evil kings who abandoned the God of Israel in favor of one of the gods of the surrounding nations—in the process leading God's people away from their destiny of holiness and blessing. Into that situation God sent the prophet Elijah to give Ahab and the children of Israel a simple choice: Who will you serve, God or Baal? Who will you allow to define your destiny, the God who created you and designed a rich and glorious future for you—or the wicked nations and people around you?

"How long will you falter between two opinions?" Elijah asked God's people. *"If the LORD is God, follow Him; but if Baal, follow him."*[4]

How often are God's people today faced with the same choice? We live in a world where there are many opposing "gods" that compete for our attention and devotion. Careers, jobs, money, relationships, and an incredible pressure to indulge in behaviors that are sinful and destructive—all of these and more steer many of those whom God loves away from the destiny He has planned for them.

Similarly, our global society with its media-molded opinions and pop-culture attitudes exerts a supremely wicked influence. Lifestyles that just a generation ago would have been considered unthinkable not only to Christians, but to society in general, are now embraced and celebrated.

---

4. 1 Kings 18:21.

Many individuals who once lived out a dynamic faith in God, and trusted in Him to guide their lives have been seduced by the gods of this world to abandon their first love, Jesus, and the rich destiny that He promises all who will follow Him. What would happen if those people were faced with the same evidence of God's power that Ahab and the children of Israel witnessed when Elijah challenged the prophets of Baal to a showdown?

As 1 Kings 18 recounts, each side—the four hundred and fifty prophets of Baal versus Elijah, the solitary prophet of the God of Israel—was given a bull to sacrifice to their deity. The God who answered with fire would be lauded as the one true God.

In this well-known story, the pathetic servants of Baal spent from early morning until evening crying themselves hoarse, cutting themselves, and making a huge spectacle as they vainly called out to their idol, trying to get it to come to life and burn up the sacrifice. After many hours of embarrassment, they finally gave up in exhaustion.

Then Elijah the prophet quietly and confidently stepped forward and called the double-minded, compromised children of Israel to watch what the true God would do. As they looked on, not even daring to hope that the God they had abandoned would show up, Elijah repaired the altar of the Lord that was broken down through years of neglect. As if to emphasize that the destiny God had planned for them was still in force if they would but turn to Him, Elijah took twelve stones—representing the twelve tribes of God's beloved Israel—and rebuilt the altar that had once stood for Israel's devotion, faith, and commitment to the God who had called them to a special purpose and plan.

Around that altar the prophet placed the wood for the fire, cut up the bull that was to be sacrificed and placed it on the altar, and then, to demonstrate that Israel served a God of the impossible, he poured twelve huge pots filled with water over the altar, finishing the preparations for the fire that Elijah was convinced God would send from heaven to demonstrate His power and might.

Finally, as the children of Israel, Ahab the evil king, and all the prophets of Baal stood by and watched doubtfully, Elijah lifted his eyes to heaven and offered a simple, heartfelt petition to God: *"Lord God of Abraham, Isaac, and Israel, let it be known this day that You are God in Israel and I am Your servant.... Hear me, O Lord...that this people may know that You are the Lord God, and that You have turned their hearts back to You again."*[5]

Scripture recounts that in response to this simple prayer, God sent down fire that not only burnt up the sacrifice, but, as if to put an exclamation point upon the glory of His presence, also consumed the wood, the stones, the dust around the altar, and all the water that had been poured over the altar.

To conclude the contest between Baal and Jehovah God, Elijah rounded up all the four hundred and fifty prophets of Baal—the men who had been so instrumental in turning the hearts of the children of Israel from the God of their destiny—and summarily executed every one of them, a bold and definitive Old Testament statement that there could be no voice of opposition or compromise if the children of Israel were to realize the destiny that God had for them.

REACHING YOUR DESTINY

Friend, the same goes for you in your quest for God's best in your life. Perhaps, like many of God's people today, you have been tempted or turned aside by the voices of this world that clamor and call you to compromise your future. Riches, fame, fortune, and the other trinkets that this world's system dangles out have threatened to turn you from total devotion to God and His plans and purposes for your life.

Or maybe you gave up a future that this world told you was bright with promise in order to follow Jesus, and now the enemy is heaping ridicule on you as you walk out your faith on a day-to-day basis.

---

5. 1 Kings 18:36–37.

You know, one of the greatest men of God, the apostle Paul, was faced with such thoughts about his past. On the one hand, Paul was no doubt dogged by remorse over the Christians he hunted down and turned over to the authorities before his life-changing encounter with Christ on the road to Damascus. Because of him, Christians were persecuted—and even killed! *Am I still responsible?* He may have wondered. On the other hand, I am sure that as he went about the often-difficult life of an apostle in the early church—with imprisonment, beatings, persecutions, and ultimately martyrdom for the cause of Christ—Paul was more than once prodded by the enemy with thoughts of the life of respect and security he might have had as an educated and hyper-religious Jew, had he never converted.

But the great apostle's response to those two sides of the enemy's attack provides you with an example to follow as you stay steadfast in your quest for God's best. He wrote, *"Forgetting those things which are behind, and reaching forth unto those things which are before, I press toward the mark for the prize of the high calling of God in Christ Jesus."*[6]

Or how about the example of the Jesus Himself? Not only was He tempted by the devil to turn away from His destiny as the Savior of all humanity, but His own brothers doubted and denigrated Him as He set His heart to do the will of His Father. Even though they had grown up around their older brother and had seen the anointing, wisdom, and divine favor upon His life, when Jesus began to do miracles among the people and multitudes thronged around Him for a touch from God, His brothers accused Him of being *"out of His mind"* and tried to stop Him.[7] A short time later, as the Jewish leaders sought to kill Him, Jesus' brothers tried to goad Him into making a public spectacle of Himself, because, as the John recounted in His gospel account, *"even His brothers did not believe in Him."*[8]

6. Philippians 3:13–14 KJV.
7. Mark 3:21.
8. John 7:5.

But Jesus would not allow anyone or anything to draw Him away from His true purpose. While circumstances, people, and Satan himself continued an unrelenting attack on Him right up to the time He died the cruel death on the cross, Jesus kept His focus on the purpose and destiny God had for Him—written before the foundation of the world.

And friend, because He remained true—suffering, dying, and rising victorious over sin, death, and all opposition to the will of God—you, too, are empowered to fulfill the destiny for which God has created you. You do not have to allow circumstances, your past, or other people to redefine that destiny. It's in His Word and it's in your heart, and all you have to do is keep your eyes turned to Him, asking Him and trusting Him to fulfill the lifetime of blessing, prosperity, and rich fulfillment for which He created you.

LEAVING *THINGS* BEHIND IS SOMETIMES THE ONLY WAY TO MOVE *YOU* FORWARD.

FAVOR
TAKEAWAY

12

THE POWER OF ASSOCIATION

Have you ever wondered why so many people who have been blessed with extraordinary opportunities in life end up squandering those opportunities and living lives of mediocrity—if not outright failure? Of course, there may be any number of reasons that people fail to wisely invest the "blessing capital" that God has set before them. But observing human nature over many years as a pastor and entrepreneur has led me to conclude that at the top of the list of reasons that individuals with the talent, intellect, and background to succeed fail to capitalize on their opportunities is that they either *did not understand* or *chose to misuse* the power of association.

You can observe this every day in the high-stakes world of collegiate and professional athletics. The stories are nearly endless of young, tremendously gifted athletes who are handed a valuable scholarship to a major university to play college basketball or football. But instead of recognizing and using that opportunity to get an education that will prepare them for a life after their day in the athletic limelight is over, they choose to coast by while keeping one foot in the past, maintaining relationships with old friends and associates who can do nothing but keep them tied to a life of destructive behaviors.

For those who make it into the pros and sign contracts for more money than they ever dreamed of making, the stakes increase exponentially, with old "friends" and hangers-on coming out of the woodwork to share in the good time and bling, pulling many of these impressionable and unprepared young millionaires into downward spirals that negatively impact their athletic abilities, squander their money, and bring emotional and relational turmoil. Some never recover.

If these young people with bright futures and destinies had had someone to guide them, helping them to plan their futures, invest their money, and discipline their lives, the paths of many would be very different. What they needed was a drastic change in who they were associating with, a reality check about who their real "friends" were.

A DIFFERENT SCENARIO

I'm reminded of a story about a young man I'll call Todd, who was gifted with an incredible ability on the football field. Todd made his high school's varsity football team as a freshman, and for the next four years was the team's star, leading his school to back-to-back state football titles. But while Todd was stellar on the field, the rest of his life was in shambles. Raised by a single mom with no father figure, Todd got in with the wrong crowd at school, began using alcohol and drugs, and had several run-ins with local law enforcement.

While his mother insisted that he spend time after school hitting the books, Todd would often slip out at night and run the streets with a crowd of "friends" who seemed determined to destroy the opportunities that presented themselves to Todd. Yet, despite barely having enough credits to graduate, not to mention a handful of arrests and incidents that sullied his record, Todd was blessed with a football scholarship to a very good school.

Unfortunately, Todd's poor choices, destructive behavior, and bad judgment in friends followed him to college. He soon found himself on academic probation and in danger of losing his scholarship and for-feiting a bright future. His college roommates were, like him, intent on having a good time at the expense of their schooling, and by the end of just a few weeks of school, not only was Todd underperforming on the field, his grades were suffering and he had been written up by his dorm dean three times for serious infractions.

It was then that Todd's college football coach stepped in. Pulling him aside after practice one day, Coach Ford informed Todd that he was being benched for the rest of the season and that, if his attitude and actions didn't improve drastically, he would be dropped from the football team and sent home. He also told Todd that he was being re-assigned to a new dorm and a new roommate, another football player by the name of Dan. "Todd, you need a healthy dose of Dan's attitude and work ethic," Coach Ford explained. "You would do well to keep your eye on him, and model a lot of what he's doing. If you don't, I'm afraid you may not be around here next season."

Dan couldn't have been more different than Todd. Quiet, seri-ous-minded, and disciplined both on and off the field, Dan was also a committed Christian who began each day with prayer and the Word of God. Additionally, Dan's friends were mostly other believers, and he ordered each day with care, discipline, and an eye to his future.

At first Todd resisted Dan's friendly manner and offhand offers to help him get his school life buttoned down. He resented Dan's quiet confidence, his faith, and the fact that he seemed to have his eye firmly fixed on his future and was working toward a goal. Before long, how-ever, Todd began to realize that what was motivating Dan and guid-ing his life was something he deeply needed. After a couple of weeks he began to get out of bed early like Dan, instead of sleeping in and missing class. He also began to hang out with Dan and his friends, and realized that they were actually just as fun as his other friends.

It also wasn't long before Todd realized that, at the core, what mo-tivated Dan was his faith in God, and the commitment of all his life to Jesus. One morning, as he joined his roommate in a morning prayer,

Dan asked Todd if he would like to make that same commitment, and Todd immediately said an emphatic "yes."

And with that personal commitment to Christ, it was as if a light switch was turned on in Todd's life.

"No, everything didn't become easy," he recalled recently, "but just knowing that I had someone I could turn to and ask for help, and a group of friends around me to help me, pray with me, cheer me on, and hold me accountable, made everything seem okay."

Not surprisingly, Todd's performance on the football field turned around, he made the Dean's List the next semester, and began working toward a goal of getting his bachelor's degree, with the plan of attending law school.

CHALLENGED TO A HIGHER LEVEL

It is not difficult to pinpoint what, exactly, caused Todd to turn the corner and begin making right choices. When he changed his associations and began hanging out with people who were going places in life, and who cared about where he was going, Todd was challenged to a higher level. Instead of having people around him who were flattering him and telling him things he wanted to hear, he now had friends who began telling him things he *needed* to hear. The book of Proverbs tells us that the wounds a true friend delivers are "*faithful*"—meaning they aren't intended to hurt but to heal.[1]

Often in the beginning, the things that Dan had to say to Todd—about drinking, neglecting his studies, staying up late, coasting at football practice instead of giving his all—made Todd angry and resentful. But he also noticed that Dan never cut him down, always had an encouraging word for him, and made it a point to include him in activities that would help Todd move in the right direction.

1. Proverbs 27:6.

"When I compared what Dan and his friends had to say to me with the things the crowd I hung out with had to say, I soon realized that Dan's group were my real friends, the ones I wanted to hang out with," Todd recalled. "In fact, I began to gauge choices I was making against what I knew Dan and his buddies would do. After a while, making better choices became nearly second nature."

NEGATIVE OR POSITIVE INFLUENCE?

One of the most effective Christian discipleship programs in the world, which has helped to turn around the lives of thousands of people caught in addictions and other life issues, requires those who enter its one-year program to lay aside contact with all but close family while they are in the program. The reason is simple: the people we associate with on a regular basis have the power to influence our attitudes and actions. Those whose lives are bound by addiction, destructive behavior, and negative attitudes most likely were introduced to those addictions, behaviors, and attitudes by someone else—and those people may still be exerting negative influence over their lives.

The apostle Paul puts it this way, telling the Corinthians that associating with the wrong people would *"corrupt"* their own behavior, morals, and character.[2] When something is corrupted, it means that it has been contaminated or poisoned, rendering it unusable until it has been cleansed and purified. Think of the city whose water supply was rendered unusable for the whole population when poison from a nearby chemical source seeped into the water source. It took months of intense cleanup before the people of that city could once again have a dependable source of clean, pure water. That's what corruption of our character is like.

Corruption is something you must be aware of in your quest for God's best in your life. The corrupting influence of the wrong friends

---

2. 1 Corinthians 15:33.

and associates can seep into your thinking, attitudes, character, and behavior, subtly robbing you of direction, momentum, and determination. If you are going to be all that God has called you to be—in your commitment to God, in your relationships, in your career path, and in every other area of life—you must distance yourself from those people who have held you back in the past.

> IF YOU ARE GOING TO BE ALL THAT GOD HAS CALLED YOU TO BE…
> YOU MUST DISTANCE YOURSELF FROM THOSE PEOPLE WHO
> HAVE HELD YOU BACK IN THE PAST.

Now, of course, there are certain relationships with family, friends, and others to which you must remain committed. Regardless of how difficult these are, God will help and empower you to live in victory above any negative influence they might have.

But if there are relationships with others that have taken their toll over the years, relationships that you know are unhealthy and keeping you from God's best, it is time for a clean break. That might mean giving up certain activities and certain places that you know will draw you into wrong behaviors. It might actually mean sacrificing things that you have enjoyed, but that you know aren't healthy—and along with leaving with the addictions, also leaving the friends who lead you into addictions.

YOU NEED LIKE-MINDED PEOPLE

A clean break may also mean limiting the amount of time you spend with people whose conversation is filled with fear, doubt, and unbelief—all attitudes that can drag you down and keep you from your destiny. For example, if God is calling you to finish college and the people you hang out with denigrate that dream, it's probably time to find new people to spend time with—people who share your dream and who cheer you on in your quest. Or if you believe God has called you into the business world, and your friends warn you that in this tough economy your business is sure to fail, that is an anchor from which you need to cut free. Such words and attitudes are diametrically opposed to God's will, His Word, and His ways!

Now when you decide to tighten up your inner circle of friends and associates and become more discriminating about who is investing emotionally and spiritually in your life, it is almost certain that you will be challenged. "Who do you think you are?" someone will ask. "Do you think you're too good to hang around with us? What's happened to you that you don't want to be with your friends anymore?"

The truth of the matter is that you owe no one an explanation. You have only one life to live, and only you are accountable before God for how you spend the years allotted to *you*. While most people live their lives by what is most convenient or comfortable, as a child of God you have a responsibility to set your sights higher, on *"things above,"* where Christ is.[3] Remember that because you are a child of God, He is Lord of your destiny, and that means He is also Lord of your associates. While God will indeed call you to speak into the lives of others and call them to a higher place, just like Dan did to Todd, God does not want you to be manipulated by those who will deliberately tear you down, and who are not on the same path toward God's best that you are.

The apostle Paul powerfully admonishes you not to be tied together in relationships with "unbelievers"—and that means anyone or any group who will not walk by the light of God's truth, which is guiding you to your destiny. *"For what fellowship has righteousness with lawlessness?"* he asks. *"And what communion has light with darkness?"*[4] If you are going to grow into all that God has called you to be in every area

3. Colossians 3:2.
4. 2 Corinthians 6:14.

of your life, you are going to have to live a life that is separated to the things of God. Those are the things that will guide you to your destiny. And that will mean hanging out with people who are like-minded, who are on the same path you are on—some further down the road, some not as far as you are, but all committed to getting there and all in need of people who will walk with them.

Friend, what I am saying is that to get to and stay in your destiny you need to be in communion both with God and with His people. If you know that the people you choose to spend time with will impact you, then wouldn't you want to be around people who are talking about faith in God, living that faith, and spending time in the Word of God—the manual for faith? Wouldn't you want to spend as much time as possible with people who spur each other on to positive attitudes, actions, and momentum, who believe that God has a plan for them—and you—that is all about blessing and prosperity?

And where is it that you will find such people with positive attitudes and dynamic destinies? The best answer to that is a church where the Word of God is preached and where you find yourself challenged to keep your expectations high and your faith strong. When you are in an atmosphere where everything that happens—from the music and preaching to the prayer and fellowship—points to God as the Source and Supplier of everything you need for life, you need look nowhere else. These are your people, and the power of associating with those who love God and love His Word will soon become evident to you.

Faith comes by hearing God's Word on a consistent basis and being encouraged to embrace His Word as the absolute truth and guide for your life. Just as darkness runs from the light, fear, doubt, and unbelief will flee from the place where Jesus is Lord and His Word is preeminent.

You will flourish and your destiny will come forth in that place where faith is welcome. If you don't know where that is, if you aren't sure where such a church exists, ask God to lead you to the right fellowship and give you encounters with like-minded people, those who will call you to a higher place, and who will be by your side each step of the way.

WHEN BELIEVERS PRAISE TOGETHER,
FAVOR IS RELEASED EXPONENTIALLY.

FAVOR
TAKEAWAY

13

EXCELLENCE AND THE POWER OF DISCIPLINE

Excellence is a popular topic these days.

In the classroom, the workplace, and throughout civic institutions and society in general, people talk about striving to be the best they can be. Seminars, self-help manuals, and experts all spouting advice on becoming better have proliferated as everyone tries to get an edge on the competition for top jobs and careers, slots in the best universities, prestigious political appointments, and positions of prominence in their communities.

But for all the talk about excellence and "personal best," it is amazing to discover how few people really understand that true excellence comes only through diligent and honest effort, focus, and determination. In fact, more than ever, people seem to be turning to shortcuts and dishonesty to get ahead. One study, for example, found that nearly 61 percent of college students confessed to having cheated on assignments and tests. And these students don't have the history you'd expect! On average those who cheat in college have the highest grade point averages. Their cheating often began in high school, and 85 percent of those who cheat think it is an important, if not essential, strategy for achieving their desired ends.[1]

It doesn't get better out in the work-a-day world. Some experts estimate that over 50 percent of job applicants lie about their background and skills on their resumes or in their cover letters to get a leg up on a job they want.[2]

And it can go as far as faking a bachelor's or advanced degree, with hundreds of college diploma "mills" around the world willing and able to print up, for a couple hundred dollars, a pretty impressive looking sheepskin that can make anyone look like a PhD in just about anything.[3]

INSTANT EVERYTHING!

In many ways this desire for people to get ahead quickly seems tied to a culture that promotes a lifestyle of instant gratification, minimal effort, and no risks. So many individuals, particularly in younger generations, have grown up with the notion that they can get just about anything they want without delay, effort, pain, setbacks, or obstacles. They have grown accustomed to screaming, "I want it now!" and having a parent or grandparent respond with an immediate answer, or having a teacher, social worker, and even their government bail them out at every turn and make their life a risk-free venture.

So if they can get a gaming system, a new pair of the latest basketball shoes, or a painless school experience with no effort, or a mere slap on the wrist and a "no big deal" mentality from authority figures

---

1. "8 Astonishing Stats on Academic Cheating," Open Education Database, December 19, 2010, http://www.oedb.org/ilibrarian/8-astonishing-stats-on-academic-cheating/ (accessed March 3, 2017).
2. Martha C. White, "You Won't Believe How Many People Lie on Their Resumes," Time.com, August 13, 2015, http://time.com/money/3995981/how-many-people-lie-resumes/ (accessed March 3, 2017).
3. Vicky Phillips, "10 Ways to Spot a Diploma Mill," GetEducated.com, https://www.geteducated.com/college-degree-mills/161-college-degree-or-diploma-mill (access March 17, 2017).

for misbehavior and even crimes, why not expect a convenient set of shortcuts to everything from a college education, thriving business, or successful career to financial independence, a happy marriage, and even a quality relationship with God?

But the truth is that there are no shortcuts to excellence and success in life. Becoming a person of true destiny—growing in and staying true to all that God has created each of us to be—requires focused and ongoing self-discipline. There are no shortcuts to what is good; there are only shortcuts to evil.

> BECOMING A PERSON OF TRUE DESTINY REQUIRES FOCUSED AND ONGOING SELF-DISCIPLINE. THERE ARE NO SHORTCUTS.

YOU WERE CREATED TO PURSUE GREATNESS

Desiring to succeed, to be the best we can be, to pursue and achieve greatness, is an inherent element in the makeup of every individual, and that desire is something that has been given to us by God. That's right! God has wired you for greatness, to reach for— and to achieve—a destiny that is beyond the mundane and every-day. When you step on to the sports field, it's a God-created spark that gives you the desire to be a champion. In school, your push to get the best grades and to be at the head of the class is divinely inspired. In your career, that drive to advance and be at the top was placed there by your Maker.

The reach for greatness was in you from the day you were conceived. It propelled you from your mother's womb, filled your lungs with the breath that caused the first cry the world heard from you. It is the divine spark that prompted the apostle Paul to boldly declare: *"I can do all things through Christ who strengthens me."*[4]

GOD HAS WIRED YOU FOR GREATNESS, TO REACH FOR—AND TO ACHIEVE—A DESTINY THAT IS BEYOND THE MUNDANE AND EVERY-DAY.

However, the motivation for greatness inside every child of God is very different from what drives the world! Jesus said that if you desire to be great in God's economy—the only place where greatness really counts—you must enter through the doorway of servanthood and humility.[5] In other words, a "me first" attitude will not fly in God's kingdom.

This is directly contrary to the world's quest for destiny. Much that drives the world today is predicated on being at the top of the heap, regardless of how one's efforts might harm someone else. While the world may give lip service to serving and sacrificing, that attitude typically comes with a "what's in it for me" disclaimer.

But that's not the way of true servant-greatness. Just think about it. Who was—and is—the greatest person who ever lived? Of course, His name is Jesus. He is the Son of God, the Creator of all things, and the One by whom all things exist. But as great and mighty as Jesus is, when He walked this earth He did not demand preeminence, nor did He strive for first place, and when His enemies opposed Him with hatred, He did not retaliate in kind. Instead, the Word of God said that He was—and is—meek and lowly, the One to whom individuals can come to find rest and peace.

---

4. Philippians 4:13.
5. See Mark 9:35.

The apostle Paul defines true greatness and the spirit of excellence by the standard of Jesus, challenging each and every child of God to embrace the mind of Christ, who voluntarily laid aside His equality with God and became a servant for all of humanity—even those who hated Him.[6] Of course, we know where that attitude led Christ—straight to the cross, where He demonstrated true servant-greatness when He laid down His life for our sins, rising victorious for our justification. Paul goes on to explain that because of Jesus' willing sacrifice, God the Father has *"highly exalted Him, and given Him the name which is above every name."*[7]

Jesus' quiet quest for the destiny that was written for Him before the foundations of the earth were even laid caused Him to set aside those attitudes and actions that define the path that most of the world takes: selfishness, worldly pleasures, and pride. Instead, Jesus applied Himself to walking humbly in the wisdom and fullness of His heavenly Father's kingdom. The Bible indicates that even as a young man Jesus was filled with wisdom and discernment, and could discuss the deep things of God with the elders of His local temple.[8]

While part of that focus certainly came from being fully God, don't forget that Jesus was tempted in all ways as we are![9] He had to fight laziness, boredom, frustration, and selfishness, just like we have to. But He lived the perfect lifestyle of discipline and preparation. The gospel accounts relate that Jesus often got up early in the morning to seek God and pray. That habit, no doubt, had begun long before his short, three-year ministry on earth began. He had honed His Spirit through diligent study of Scripture, long hours spent in God's presence, and a lifestyle of humility and servanthood. They prepared Him for the cross.

---

6. See Philippians 2:5–7.
7. Philippians 2:9.
8. See Luke 2:46–47.
9. See Hebrews 4:15.

TAKING HIS YOKE UPON YOU

The same self-discipline and God-focus that defined the life, death, and resurrection of our Lord Jesus Christ is the path to your own greatness and excellence. In fact, Jesus offers an invitation to self-discipline. He says that whoever will follow Him must "*deny himself.*" Whoever seeks to save his or her own life will really lose it, but whoever loses their life through surrender to Jesus and the way of the cross will find true greatness and destiny.[10]

How can you "*deny yourself*"? It all comes back to discipline. If you are going to fulfill all that God has created you to be, you will do so through the doorway of disciplining your heart, mind, and efforts to His way—the way of surrender. When Jesus invites you to "take His yoke" upon you, He is really inviting you to embrace your destiny in Him. "Learn from me," He says, "for I am meek, humble, and servant-like, and in coming under My yoke of surrender and discipline, you will not only find your destiny, but it will come with an abundance of peace."[11]

When God created you and placed within you a destiny and purpose, He knew that it could only come through the order of His kingdom, rather than the chaos and confusion of what the world calls progress.

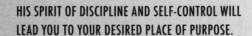

HIS SPIRIT OF DISCIPLINE AND SELF-CONTROL WILL
LEAD YOU TO YOUR DESIRED PLACE OF PURPOSE.

---

10. Luke 9:23–24.
11. See Matthew 11:29–30.

Too many of God's people are trying to find their destiny in that system, which is filled with anxiety, stress, fear, and failure. By contrast, God said that He has not given us that spirit. Rather, His guiding principles in our lives is one of power, of His love, and of self-discipline. His Spirit of discipline and self-control will lead you to your desired place of purpose.

ACCEPT NO SUBSTITUTES!

Friend, even as many of those around you are busy striving for greatness on the world's dead-end path, I want to invite you to take the route of God's discipline, applying yourself diligently to know Him through daily time in the Word, active prayer, ongoing surrender to His will, and a humble servant attitude in your daily lifestyle. Such a heart posture will actually empower and position you to excel in the earthly destiny for which God has created you. Just as Daniel, Shadrach, Meshach, and Abednego refused to follow the world's methods and were rewarded by God for their diligence and self-discipline, your choice to disencumber yourself from the attitudes and lifestyle of the world will position you for greatness and destiny in God's kingdom.

The apostle John encourages you as God's child not to love the world or the things in it, because it is all passing away. Set your heart, instead, on God's kingdom, which lasts forever.[12] Applying your heart to know and follow God's Word will position you to take your place in that eternal kingdom as well.

John W. Gardner, a noted expert on leadership, observed that while an individual might occasionally be thrown into a situation that places the mark of greatness upon him or her, few people indeed "have excellence thrust upon them. They achieve it. They do not achieve it unwittingly by 'doing what comes naturally,' and they don't stumble into it in the course of amusing themselves." Inevitably, despite the

---

12. 1 John 2:15–17.

shortcuts that people attempt, all excellence, observed Gardner, "involves discipline and tenacity of purpose."[13]

My sincere advice to you, dear friend, is to accept no shortcuts or substitutes in your quest for God's greatness and destiny in your life. The apostle Paul wrote that while there may be many runners in a race, the prize for first place will only go to the one who has put his or her *all* into the discipline of preparation.[14] In the dreams and destiny you are pursuing—from finishing your education and succeeding in a career or business, to your relationship with God and every area of your personal life—make *godly excellence* your goal. Pray for it, pursue it, surround yourself with those who will help you get there, and help others get there as well, with an attitude of a humble servant.

---

13. John W. Gardner, *Excellence* (New York: W. W. Norton & Company, 1995), 76.
14. See 1 Corinthians 9:24.

EXCELLENCE IS ALWAYS POSSIBLE
FOR ANYONE WHO DENIES HIM- OR HERSELF.

FAVOR
TAKEAWAY

14

THE POWER OF GIVING

Two brothers were sitting at the kitchen table with the last two pieces of their mother's delicious apple pie from the previous night's dinner. The older brother proceeded to serve himself the larger piece of pie, leaving a much smaller serving for his frustrated younger sibling.

"You're sure not a very good Christian example," the younger brother challenged as the older boy settled in to enjoy his piece of pie.

"What do you mean?" replied the older brother, pretending not to know what his brother was talking about.

"The Bible says that it's better to give than to receive," the younger boy responded, "but you took the bigger piece of Mom's pie without even asking which one I wanted."

The savvy older brother thought for a moment, then, with a twinkle in his eye, asked, "Which piece would you have taken?"

"I would have let you have the bigger piece," the younger brother said with self-righteous indignation.

"Well," replied the older brother, "what are you complaining about? That's the one I've got!"

GIVING OR RECEIVING—WHICH IS BETTER?

That little anecdote offers a light-hearted demonstration of how many individuals approach the blessing-opportunity of giving. The majority of people in our culture give enthusiastic lip service to the words of Jesus quoted by the apostle Paul: *"It is more blessed to give than to receive."*[1] And our world even displays some high-profile examples of corporate charity and giving, where community action takes hold and people dig in to make sure homeless shelters stay open, food pantries have enough of the basics to keep the poor fed, and community clothes closets are stocked with sufficient hand-me-downs to provide for the destitute.

But when you take a closer look at much large-scale benevolence, you find the charity that people perform is usually done out of their surplus and overflow. In other words, they are making sure that they and theirs have both their wants and their needs met—as well as the luxuries—before they give their "fair share" to the needs of others. Much of the giving we see in society is done out of the spirit that motivated the two brothers in the above illustration: people will give to the needs of others, as long as they get the first—and largest—blessing.

PEOPLE WILL GIVE TO THE NEEDS OF OTHERS, AS LONG AS THEY GET THE FIRST—AND LARGEST—BLESSING.

1. Acts 20:35.

Now please hear me when I say that such efforts are good and should be vigorously encouraged! Millions of people have been helped over the years by community charities funded by individuals, families, and businesses.

But I don't believe that giving out of our surplus and overflow was what was in Jesus' heart when He challenged His disciples that God's richest blessings come on the giving end rather than the receiving end.

The apostle Paul, who was using Jesus' words to spur leaders in the Ephesus church to take care of the needs of those in their community of believers, provides one of the best examples of what godly, impactful giving is all about. As this chief man of God fulfilled his historic destiny by planting, growing, and nurturing churches throughout the world, he funded his God-commissioned venture by working as a tentmaker. In other words, he worked a day job to fund the true destiny God had for him. Not only did he provide for his own needs by working with his hands so that he could do the work of the gospel, but he actually also provided for those around him! He provided for the needs of his coworkers in the gospel outreach, as well as for those to whom he ministered, many of whom were in dire straits and terribly wanting for the basics of life.

The reason? Paul was providing an example for those to whom he ministered, showing that through hard work, diligence, and self-sacrifice, they too were called to help those in need, giving freely of their time, talents, and resources. Jesus put it this way: *"Heal the sick, cleanse the lepers, raise the dead, cast out devils: freely ye have received, freely give."*[2]

Those words—*"freely ye have received, freely give"*—are foundational to tapping into the heart of godly giving. For you see, benevolence has no value in and of itself. As hard as it is to say this, all those people who give freely to the needs of others, but who have no faith in Christ Jesus as Savior and Lord—are really giving in vain, because

2. Matthew 10:8 KJV.

their giving is not tied to the true giver of eternal life. In order to be an empowered giver, you must first be a receiver of God's mercy and grace into your own life. Only at that point can you "freely give," and it is at that point that God will pour back into your life the things you need to step into your destiny.

How far have God's people drifted from Christ's mandate for those who would find their destiny in Him! Today, for much of the church in our culture, following Jesus means little more than an occasional Bible study, church attendance when convenient, and some half-hearted, begrudging giving of one's financial resources.

But for all those to dare to "give freely" out of what they have received, God reserves a special gift and grace.

> FOR ALL THOSE TO DARE TO "GIVE FREELY" OUT OF WHAT THEY HAVE RECEIVED, GOD RESERVES A SPECIAL GIFT AND GRACE.

THE NOBILITY OF GODLY GIVING

There is an old French saying, *noblesse oblige*, which translates to "the nobility is obligated." Historically, there was an expectation that those blessed with title, wealth, power, and prestige had a *responsibility* to use those blessings for the good of those less fortunate. The *nobility* was *obligated* to do so. In ancient and medieval times, a king, queen, or person of nobility, who had the means to do so, was expected to use his or her power, influence, and resources in a way that helped others who were not as blessed. Likewise, in more recent eras, and in our own time, many business people, industrialists, and those of wealth and influence have considered it an *obligation* to use their wealth and means for more than just their own personal comfort.

That is the motivation behind the high-profile philanthropy carried out today by such wealthy and influential people as the Rockefeller family, Oprah Winfrey, and rock star Bono. One notable example is Microsoft billionaire Bill Gates, who with his wife, Melinda, has donated at least $28 billion to the foundation bearing their name. Over the past years the Bill and Melinda Gates Foundation has given billions of dollars to help the poor around the world through agriculture, health, and other global assistance programs. Explaining the motivation behind his generosity, Mr. Gates recalled that his mother, herself a successful businesswoman, "never stopped pressing me to do more for others. A few days before my wedding, she hosted a bridal event, at which she read aloud a letter about marriage that she had written to Melinda. Although ill with cancer at the time, she saw just one more opportunity to deliver her message, and at the close of the letter she wrote: 'From those to whom much is given, much is expected.'"[3] Mrs. Gates' strong, motivational message to her son was that because he had been blessed with so much—education, opportunity, wealth, and influence—he had a special obligation to make sure that he used each of those blessings for the betterment of his fellow human beings.

Whether or not Bill Gates' mother realized it, the powerful counsel she gave her son is actually scriptural. Jesus emphasized to His disciples that those whose destinies are marked by Christ's redemption, who are the recipients of all that He purchased through His death and resurrection, have a heightened responsibility to those around them to be salt and light and pour out the mercy that they have freely received. As blood-bought children of God, we do not have the right to sit back on our heels while people around us are suffering in sin,

---

3. Bill Gates, "Remarks of Bill Gates, Harvard Commencement 2007," *Harvard Gazette*, June 7, 2007, http://news.harvard.edu/gazette/story/2007/06/remarks-of-bill-gates-harvard-commencement-2007/ (accessed March 3, 2017).

sickness, poverty, and oppression. *"For unto whomsoever much is given,"* Jesus told His disciples, *"of him shall be much required."*[4]

The apostle Peter reminds us that we are *"chosen generation, a royal priesthood, a holy nation, His own special people."*[5] As God's children through Jesus Christ we are "royalty," and we have responsibilities that come with such a title and privilege. We are set apart to show forth His mercy and faithfulness to the rest of the world, particularly to those in deep need.

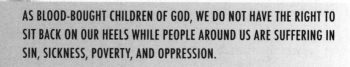

AS BLOOD-BOUGHT CHILDREN OF GOD, WE DO NOT HAVE THE RIGHT TO SIT BACK ON OUR HEELS WHILE PEOPLE AROUND US ARE SUFFERING IN SIN, SICKNESS, POVERTY, AND OPPRESSION.

GIVE LIKE GOD DOES!

Have you ever observed someone who was "born to wealth," a person raised in a lifestyle of luxury and financial comfort? Such a person exhibits no concern over issues of want or lack, and is as free in how he spends money on others as he is in how he spends it on himself. Such an individual has an inherent understanding that the wealth of his father is also at his command, and if he has a need, all he has to do is go to Dad and ask.

Friend, you have just such a relationship with your heavenly Father. In case you somehow forgot, He owns the cattle on a thousand hills,[6] and He has the wealth of the universe at His disposal. He has also promised that He will supply all your needs abundantly

---

4. Luke 12:48 KJV.
5. 1 Peter 2:9.
6. See Psalm 50:10.

out of His limitless storehouse.[7] Yes, your heavenly Father is extravagant with His wealth, and He expects you, as a child "born to wealth," to behave in a way that is fitting with your wealth and position. Where need exists, God expects His people to step forward with the answer, sometimes individually, sometimes corporately through the church or some other faith group, but always with faith, boldness, and the assurance that this is part and parcel of their destiny as God's children.

How is it, then, that so many of God's children suffer from a good old-fashioned case of stinginess? Could it be that they are not convinced of God's goodness? I have actually found that as God blesses people with wealth and prosperity, instead of responding in kind by giving back into His kingdom, many believers grow cautious and pull back on their generosity. I read a study a while back showing that as people's income grows they have a tendency to give away a smaller and smaller percentage.

I'm reminded of a story about a young man who prayed for a job, and when God answered he responded a couple weeks later by presenting his pastor with a crisp fifty-dollar bill, ten percent of his first pay check, and making a promise that he would continue giving 10 percent of his income. God continued to bless this young man so that in the next few years his monthly tithe grew to a thousand dollars. One Sunday the young man came to church and sheepishly told the pastor that because he was so successful and making so much money, he thought 10 percent of his income was a little steep for him to pay every month. "I have more expenses than ever," he complained, "and I really think 10 percent is a little more than I can give. I'd like to reduce my giving to five percent. That's still $500 a month!" Without missing a beat the pastor responded, "Young man, tithing 10 percent of your income is a biblical principle, and you did make a promise. But I think God can meet you halfway. I'm going to pray that God reduces your income so that you can comfortably manage that $500 tithe!"

---

7. See Philippians 4:19.

YOUR DESTINY IS TO GIVE

That wise pastor gave the young businessman a quick lesson in the economics of God's kingdom, which is founded on an open hand and an open heart. God does not look at our bank accounts to see how much we are to give. Everything we have is His, and His desire is for us to give it back to Him freely, with the expectation that He will supply our needs abundantly.

That, no doubt, was the motivation of the woman whom Jesus saw casting two small, insignificant copper coins into the collection at the Jerusalem temple. As Jesus sat and observed, He watched many wealthy people put in vastly more than the poor woman's two mites. Yet He declared that the woman had, in reality, given *more* than all of the rest, because the others had given out of their wealth and abundance, but the woman had given everything she had, holding nothing back.[8]

Do you get the picture here? Whether you are person of vast wealth and influence, as poor as the proverbial church mouse, or somewhere in between, your destiny is to be a giver—a *real* giver, not one who merely doles sparingly out of his surplus. If you are a child of God, trusting in His provision and fully surrendered to His will, then God's will is for you to give largely, liberally, extravagantly. And in return, He promises you an ongoing prosperity, not just for your own needs, but to continue in even greater giving to God's kingdom.

Now hear me, God is faithful to give back to you either way. If you decide that all you can do is to give sparingly, then God's blessing back to you will be meager and spare. But if you purpose in your heart always to dig a little deeper and give a little more where you see a need, God promises that the return to you will be *"good measure, pressed down, shaken together, and running over."*[9]

---

8. See Mark 12:44.
9. Luke 6:38.

YOUR HEAVENLY BANK ACCOUNT

Since 2008, there has been a worldwide shift in peoples' attitudes regarding money and financial security. Many have deep concerns about the future of our economy, and many are wondering if they will have a job and a dependable source of income in the future. However, while those concerns have prompted fear and alarm for the world at large, I have observed that for an increasing number of *God's* people, such winds of change have caused them instead to turn their hearts away from earthly treasure, to seek God more intently, and to simplify their lifestyles so that they can pour a greater part of their time, talents, and resources into the work of the kingdom.

It's beautiful!

Instead of allowing the fears that drive the world to grip them, they have taken to heart God's promise that He will take care of them, and Jesus' counsel to *"lay up"* their treasure in heaven, rather than on earth, where it will soon pass away.[10] In short, ever more of God's people are choosing to turn away from pursuing the "American dream" so that they can fix their hearts on a heavenly vision of giving their all to the call of God's kingdom.

Friend, there is something liberating in letting go once and for all of the cares and distractions of this world, and of coming to the realization that our opportunity in life to reach our destiny in Christ is brief. Such was the realization of early-American Quaker missionary Stephen Grellet, who penned these immortal words: "I expect to pass through this world but once. Any good, therefore, that I can do or any kindness I can show to any fellow creature, let me do it now. Let me not defer or neglect it, for I shall not pass this way again."[11]

Friend, can you see how such an attitude should be at the heart of your pursuit of God's best for your life? Jesus said that if you want to

10. Matthew 6:19–21.
11. Attributed to Stephen Grellet (1773–1855).

be great in God's kingdom, learn to be the *"servant of all."*[12] The best, most effective servant is the one who has purposed in his heart to give unconditionally and without restraint until he can give no more. That, of course, describes the servant heart of Christ, and it ought to define the giving of each of God's children.

TREASURE IN HEAVEN, ABUNDANCE NOW

The Word of God says that one day each one of us will appear before the judgment seat of Christ, to give an account for all that we did while we were on earth. While we are saved by the blood of Jesus Christ through His mercy and grace alone, we will nonetheless be called to answer for our actions, motives, and heart condition as His servants on this earth.[13] How will those of God's children answer their Lord, who spent their time, talents, and resources laying up treasure on earth, while ignoring their heavenly bank account? The apostle Paul tells us that, yes, they will be saved, but *"as through fire,"* all of their earthly, temporal treasures burned up and destroyed by God's holy, refining fire.[14]

Yes, on that eternal day there will be some Christians who stand before their Lord in shame and regret as they realize that all they lived for on this earth—wealth, possessions, reputation, and honor among men—is gone, burned up as worthless.

But there will be others who hear the words as they stand before Christ: *"Well done, good and faithful servant."*[15] They will be the ones who have invested their time, talents, and resources into the wealth and work of God's unshakeable, unending kingdom. Their treasure will be the gold, silver, and precious stones of souls brought to salvation, the hungry fed, the poor cared for, those in prison visited and ministered to.

---

12. Mark 9:35.
13. See 2 Corinthians 5:10.
14. 1 Corinthians 3:15.
15. Matthew 25:21.

God's Word declares that the seeds we sow in this world will bear a harvest. What we invest here and now will pay a dividend. If our sowing is done in selfishness with little thought of God's eternal economy, then what we reap will all pass away and be lost. But if our sowing is done with an eye to eternity, the Bible declares that we will reap a harvest of *"everlasting life"*—not just for ourselves, but for our friends, loved ones, and the untold individuals into whose lives we poured the resources with which God supplied us.[16]

Beloved, my prayer is that you will embrace the true heart of godly giving, so that on the day you stand before your Lord, you will not be ashamed, but will rejoice at the treasure you have laid up for all eternity. And be assured that God is faithful to provide abundantly for your needs in this life as well. He has promised to supply *"all your need"* richly and abundantly.[17] It's a win-win situation for those who will trust in God: abundant prosperity here *and* in eternity!

16. Galatians 6:7–8.
17. Philippians 4:19.

GIVING IS THE BEST WAY
TO RECEIVE.

FAVOR
TAKEAWAY

15

HANDLING REJECTION

If you have committed yourself to following God without hesitation, and have determined to see the destiny He has for you unfold completely in your life, then one thing is certain: such a decision will cause you to face your share of rejection, hurt, and offense.

The reason is simple. Most people in this world do not operate on the principles that guide God's kingdom, and thus most people they will not understand or tolerate your focus on faith and obedience to God and His Word. While some may give lip service to faith, and may initially cheer you on in your desire to walk with God and see His glory unfold in your life, when they see the lengths to which you will go to follow your convictions, most will reject your consecration.

Remember, Jesus said that whoever does not deny himself or herself, take up their cross (in other words, to let go of all hindrances, distractions, and selfish ambition), and follow Him unreservedly is not worthy to be His disciple. This vital Scripture has not been taught and heeded much in the church over the years, and it is a difficult concept for those who are used to a message of easy grace. So when someone steps forward who is willing to declare, "I will find my destiny in

His will alone, not mine," that person will be rejected by many, even other Christians.

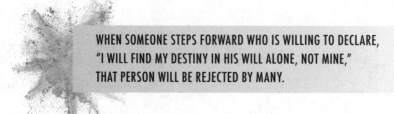

> WHEN SOMEONE STEPS FORWARD WHO IS WILLING TO DECLARE, "I WILL FIND MY DESTINY IN HIS WILL ALONE, NOT MINE," THAT PERSON WILL BE REJECTED BY MANY.

JESUS WAS DESPISED AND REJECTED

Jesus Himself was the most rejected man in all of history. Isaiah 53:3, one of the prophetic Scriptures that looked ahead to Jesus over seven hundred years before His birth, foretells that Christ would be *"despised and rejected,"* that He would be *"a Man of sorrows and acquainted with grief,"* and that even those called to be His people would despise Him and refuse to give Him honor and esteem.

Recall that during Jesus' earthly ministry, throngs initially followed Him because of the mighty miracles that He did. But when His teaching became difficult and turned to the issue of obedience and the true nature of why He came—to deny Himself and die so that others could follow Him in the same lifestyle of sacrifice and servanthood—Scripture recounts that many of those who started out as His disciples turned away and followed Him no more.[1]

And recall that Jesus entered Jerusalem to a crowd of adoring people crying out, *"Blessed is He who comes in the name of the LORD,"*[2] but within days, He faced the lonely road to Golgotha and the cross, rejected by nearly everyone who had followed and worshiped Him. Jesus Himself warned His disciples that they would face rejection by

---

1. See John 6:66.
2. Matthew 21:9.

those who claimed to be God's people. "I'm telling you these things in advance so you won't be surprised and offended when they come to pass," He told the twelve. "They will throw you out of their assemblies and congregations, and the time will even come when they will kill you and think they are doing God a favor."[3]

THE PRICE OF YOUR DESTINY

Friend, if the world treated Christ and His early disciples with disregard and rejection, don't be surprised when you are rejected—by friends and associates, by family, and even by some fellow Christians—for your choice to believe God, obey Him whatever the cost, and trust Him totally for the unfolding of your destiny, instead of pursuing the world's path to success.

The good news is that Jesus has promised you His Holy Spirit, His perfect counsel, and His help in your quest for His best in your life. He will never leave you nor will He forsake you, and He has promised to give you good success as you continue in His Word and will.

Be of good cheer, because Jesus has gone before you and has already overcome all the obstacles that you will face. He rose victorious over the world and all the enemy can throw at you so that, with the eyes of your spirit fixed firmly on Him, you can be victorious in all to which God has called you.

THE PAIN—AND PURPOSE—OF REJECTION

Yes, rejection from others, particularly from those whose affirmation we value, is inevitably painful, but it can serve a crucial role in preparing and grounding us for God's best in our lives. God can use rejection to toughen and temper us, to turn our eyes away from an unhealthy need for the approval of loved ones or personal heroes. He might even use it to move us into a new and exciting chapter in our

---

3. See John 16:1–2.

faith adventure. Afterward, we'll look back and think, *Without that rejection, I would never have turned in the new direction.*

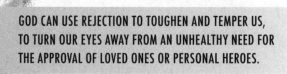

GOD CAN USE REJECTION TO TOUGHEN AND TEMPER US, TO TURN OUR EYES AWAY FROM AN UNHEALTHY NEED FOR THE APPROVAL OF LOVED ONES OR PERSONAL HEROES.

I am reminded of the compelling story of a man named William Seymour, who lived in the early part of the twentieth century, and whom God used mightily to usher in one of the greatest spiritual revivals in modern church history. The son of African slaves and blind in one eye, William Seymour struggled with a sense of inferiority as he purposed to move into the ministry to which God had called him.

In 1905 he moved to Houston, Texas, and was powerfully impacted by the ministry of Charles Parham, a minister whom God was using to usher in an experience somewhat new to the American church called the baptism of the Holy Spirit. After being taught in Parham's Bible school, Seymour was called to Los Angeles to pastor a little storefront church that was seeking more of God's holiness and power.

The Reverend Seymour was excited to minister to this new little congregation and to tell them about the power and authority that was available to all believers who would yield themselves to the Holy Spirit.

But after just one service Pastor Seymour was tersely told to leave because his message of God's movement was not welcome in the little church.

Devastated by the rejection from his new congregation, but undeterred in what he knew was God's direction, Brother Seymour made his way to the home of a hospitable family from church who offered to take him in. There, this man of God gave himself to fasting and prayer for God's next step. Before long, not only did the family where he was staying join Brother Seymour in seeking God, but others came alongside as well.

Soon the spontaneous meeting moved to a nearby home in Los Angeles, where God showed up with the powerful outpouring of the Holy Spirit which Brother Seymour had hoped would come through the little church that had rejected him. Ultimately the group moved to a broken-down building at 312 Azusa Street in Los Angeles, and a powerful revival broke out—the Azusa Street Revival. It was a God-ordained move of the Holy Spirit that has impacted hundreds of millions of individuals across the earth and continues to this day with signs, wonders, and an ongoing breath of God's Spirit across the globe.

Friend, I am sure that this humble man of God, William Seymour, had little idea of the massive, miraculous move of God that the rejection by his new little church would spark. At first he only knew the pain and disappointment of being turned aside in his passionate commitment to obey God and fulfill his destiny. How sad it would have been had he let that rejection negatively impact him through bitterness or unforgiveness! Had Brother Seymour held a grudge against those who turned him out of his church after one service, or had he bad-mouthed the congregation or individuals to others, it is highly unlikely that God would have chosen this simple, humble, unassuming man of God. God would most likely have found another vessel through whom to pour out the impacting, earth-shaking move of His Holy Spirit.

Some of the first individuals impacted by the fresh breeze of God's Spirit that resulted from Brother Seymour's obedience and humility were members of that very congregation. You see, they were hungry for God's move also, and that rejection, which came from the hands of one or two leading church members, was the catalyst for something larger God had planned.

LOOK TO HIS PROMISE

In your own life you have most likely already faced rejection, hurts, misunderstandings, and disappointments in your quest for God's best. Maybe the job promotion you were so certain was God's answer to prayer went to someone else instead. Or maybe the university you had your heart set on and had worked so diligently to be accepted into, rejected you. Perhaps someone you trusted and whose affirmation you really thought you needed, suddenly turned their back on you. Or perhaps your family, friends, or fellow believers have advised you to tone down your passion for the things of God and for seeing His glory and power raised high in your community. Or maybe it's just that others have not recognized your efforts and achievements in your journey toward fulfilling your dream and destiny.

I'm reminded of the story of a seasoned woman of God long ago who had spent many years on a foreign mission field, serving tirelessly for the kingdom of God. Finally it was time for her to come home, and so she got on a huge ocean vessel that sailed for America. It was a lonely journey, but she looked forward to getting home and seeing old friends and loved ones. She quietly hoped that a few of them might be waiting to welcome her when the ship sailed into port. There happened to be a famous movie star sailing to America on the same ship, and when the vessel arrived at the port, thousands of fans crowded the pier, clamoring and cheering his arrival. News reporters fawned over him and celebrated his latest success.

But as the elderly woman of God stepped off the ship and scanned the crowds, she saw no one waiting for her. No one was there to welcome her home and celebrate her long years of tireless devotion to the kingdom of God. "Lord, is there no one who remembers me, who cares for the work I have done for You all these years?" the woman complained. "Didn't You remind anyone to welcome me home?"

Before the godly but disappointed woman had finished uttering her heart's complaint, the Lord spoke to her in His love and wisdom, "I am here to welcome you. And besides, you're not home yet."

Friend, when you get weary of the disappointments, rejection, hurts, and misunderstandings that will inevitably come to you when you throw your all into the Lord's plan for your life, be assured that the God is watching you, in your strengths and victories and in your weakness and defeats. He is your greatest champion and supporter, and He will never reject or turn away your efforts to please Him and move further toward your destiny. When He calls you home, be assured that you will be met with great rejoicing.

YOUR FUTURE BEGINS WITH FORGIVENESS

As I have faced hurt and rejection, I have come up with a simple formula to help me successfully navigate through those disappointments and buffetings, and to come out on the other side with a clear perspective on my future. These three elements have given me the determination to step forward into the next chapter and phase of God's plan for my life. I believe they will be just as powerful in your journey.

FORGIVENESS

The first step is *forgiveness*, something we all need a whole lot of. Remember, friend, that to reach for the prize of God's high calling, you must get rid of all baggage that will hold you back. And there is no greater weight that will hold you back than unforgiveness. Jesus is clear about that! When He taught His disciples to pray, one of the key elements of that prayer was a request for God's forgiveness. *"Forgive us our debts as we forgive our debtors,"* goes this memorable petition in the Lord's Prayer.[4] Jesus emphasized that it is essential for us to release

---

4. Matthew 6:12.

others from their trespasses against us in order for us to receive the full forgiveness God has promised to give us. "For if you forgive others for their sins against you, your heavenly Father will also forgive you," Jesus is essentially saying. "But if you do not forgive others, neither will your Father forgive you."

Recall the parable that Jesus told about the man who owed a king ten thousand talents.[5] The king called the unfortunate man to him and demanded full payment immediately. The king quickly discovered that the debt was more than the man would earn in several lifetimes, so he ordered that the man and his entire family be sold into slavery so that he could at least get a small token of what was owed to him. But the man fell at the king's feet and begged for mercy, telling him that if the king gave him time, he would try to pay all that he owed. It was a ridiculous claim, but the king was so taken aback with compassion that he instantly forgave the man all his debt.

Now you would think that this man who had just been given his life back would be equally forgiving to those who owed him money. But in the parable, Jesus relates that this ungrateful man went out and found a fellow servant who owed him a sum that was only a tiny fraction of what he had been forgiven, and demanded full payment immediately. When his fellow servant begged for mercy, this wicked man instead threw him into prison until he had paid every last penny.

You probably know the ending. The king found out what had happened, called the wicked man to him, and asked, "I forgave all your debt when you asked me. Could you not have done the same for the one who owed you?" And he threw the unforgiving servant into prison until he had paid him all that he owed.

Then Jesus puts a severe exclamation point on the parable, addressed to each one of us: *"So My heavenly Father also will do to you if each of you, from his heart, does not forgive his brother his trespasses."*[6]

---

5. See Matthew 18:21–35.
6. Matthew 18:35.

Friend, the truth is that we could never repay the debt we owe as sinners. But Christ stepped in and paid the price for us, reconciling us to God and opening the door to a rich and joyous destiny. How sad it is, then, when any of us, who has been forgiven so greatly, holds a debt of bitterness or unforgiveness over someone else's head!

I want to exhort you right now to take some time to consciously, emphatically forgive in your heart any person you feel has wronged you, from a spouse or other family member, to an employer or other individual who may have dealt wrongly with you. Declare your forgiveness of that person and ask God to help that forgiveness in any way necessary. Ask Him to make the wrong things right—and then leave it in His hands to complete.

FAITH

Having taken that important step of forgiveness, the next step to overcoming hurts and embracing God's best is to *declare your faith* in God's goodness and future for you. We know that without faith it is impossible to please God, but even just a minute amount—a mustard seed, Jesus said—will change a situation. Truthfully, God responds enthusiastically when His people declare their faith in Him. So even in the depths of disappointments and hurt, if you will declare His goodness, you will be surprised by the results. David said he would have fainted unless he had believed that He would see the goodness of the Lord in the land of the living.[7]

> GOD RESPONDS ENTHUSIASTICALLY WHEN HIS PEOPLE DECLARE THEIR FAITH IN HIM.

7. See Psalm 27:13.

A response of faith in our lives takes two actions: believing and confessing. The Bible says that with the heart one believes and with the mouth one confesses.[8] Now, of course, the apostle Paul is speaking about the act of salvation in this verse, but in reality, believing and confessing are important in every aspect of your faith walk.

I have learned that in my most vulnerable times of facing hurts and disappointments, it is important to cling to God's Word and declare it—regardless of how I feel or what my emotions tell me. Some of my greatest victories have come when I was at my lowest ebb emotionally and even spiritually. The simple act of obeying God's Word and declaring it over my brokenness, pain, and disappointment has made the difference, and I have watched circumstances change in an instant.

You can expect the same results as you declare your confidence in God's goodness in your life, even in the face of hurts and disappointment. Look to the Psalms for a wealth of confidence-building Scriptures; I have often found myself digging into the depths of this book for a simple declarative statement of faith. On many occasions in his life David was faced with, hurt, rejection, and disappointment at the hands of others—often people whom he had trusted and to whom he had been deeply loyal. Yet despite the changing ways of man, David found he could always rest in God. The Psalms are a declaration of the hope he found in his loving heavenly Father. *"Trust in the* LORD *and do good,"* declared David, *"delight yourself in the* LORD *and He shall give you the desires of your heart. Commit your way to the Lord, trust also in Him, and He shall bring it to pass. He shall bring forth your righteousness as the light, and your justice as the noonday."*[9]

FORTITUDE

The third element is fortitude. Now that's not a word we hear very much nowadays, but I like the noble ring it has. As Christians

---

8. See Romans 10:10.
9. Psalm 37:3–6.

we have the very essence of nobility within us: the character of Christ. Fortitude—or courage—is one of those qualities we are called to embrace, and with it we can successfully challenge the hurt, rejection, and offense that every child of God faces at some time in his or her quest for God's best. Friend, with the authority of Christ you are empowered to stand in courage against every false accusation, offense, or opposition you face.

Remember that following Moses' death Joshua took over as the leader of the children of Israel, and as they stood ready to enter the Promised Land, God reinforced the stance of courage that Joshua and Caleb had taken a generation earlier. *"Have I not commanded you?"* God declared to Joshua. *"Be strong and of a good courage. Do not be afraid, nor be dismayed, for the LORD your God is with you wherever you go."*[10]

The Lord is declaring the same thing to you today. Like the children of Israel, you will face plenty of obstacles, offense, and rejection by those around you. There will be plenty of warfare for you to wage, using prayer and God's Word as your weapons. But if you will keep your heart ever tuned to God's Word and His Spirit, you will hear God calling you to courage and fortitude. "Do not fear, for I am with you." You will hear your heavenly Father say to you, "Do not be dismayed, because I alone am your God. I will strengthen you, help you, and uphold you with the right hand of My righteousness."[11]

YOUR DESTINY IS ASSURED

Child of God, hold your head up and look to your source! He will never forsake you, even in those times that the rejection of others presses against you. You have been imbued with a power from on high that will take you to that desired place of God's best for you. Stay strong and in faith, looking ever to the Word of God for your assurance.

10. See Joshua 1:9.
11. See Isaiah 41:10.

CHILD OF GOD, HOLD YOUR HEAD UP
AND LOOK TO YOUR SOURCE! HE WILL NEVER FORSAKE YOU.

With a heart filled with *forgiveness* toward those who have wronged and rejected you; with *faith* in God's Word and an unshakeable assurance that He who began a good work in you will complete it; and with a stance of Holy-Spirit-empowered *fortitude*, you are walking victoriously and will possess every good thing God has reserved just for you in His heavenly storehouse.

YOUR PAST PAIN IS NEVER STRONGER
THAN GOD'S PRESENT PLAN.

FAVOR
TAKEAWAY

16

EMBRACE EVERY SEASON OF LIFE

Susan is a successful attorney and partner in a thriving law firm. She is also a popular mentor to high school and college students preparing for their futures. She remembers that time in her own life vividly:

> I enjoy working with the young men and women with hopes, dreams, and ambitions for their future. They remind me so much of when I was their age, with all the confidence that I could conquer the world quickly and be at the top of my career in no time. Just like many of these talented young people today, I was restless and impatient for success, and it took me a while to understand the importance of embracing each season that God placed before me to walk through. That is one thing I try to instill in those I coach and mentor: God's best for us comes through the seasons of life, and He wants us to enjoy and embrace each valuable chapter in the story He has created for us, even as we anticipate the great things He has planned for our futures.

GOD'S BEST FOR US COMES THROUGH THE SEASONS OF LIFE, AND HE WANTS US TO ENJOY AND EMBRACE EACH VALUABLE CHAPTER IN THE STORY HE HAS CREATED FOR US.

THE BLESSED LIFE

Like many successful people, Susan worked hard for many years to reach the place of influence she holds today. "In high school I learned early on that I wouldn't be able to coast through on intelligence alone," she explained. "I had to work hard for every grade I got, and I realized that college wouldn't be any easier. I determined that I would commit myself to whatever process God placed me in to reach the goals He had for me, and always put forth my best effort."

In addition to working diligently in the classroom, Susan worked a series of jobs throughout college and even law school. "For the first two years of college I worked nights and weekends at a fast food restaurant," she recounted. "I was so embarrassed when some of my classmates came in and saw me behind the counter. I thought it was demeaning to have to work a job like that, and I looked forward to the day when I could leave that atmosphere and my coworkers and move on in my dreams."

But a curious thing happened in Susan's heart after she had, indeed, moved on in her life.

I began to look back on those early years when long days of school, low-paying jobs, and lots of struggles were the norm, and I suddenly realized that those were some of the best days of my life, and very foundational to the success I enjoy today. Sure, there were many difficult times, but those difficulties taught me perseverance and to hold on to the vision God gave me for my future. They also helped me to enjoy simple things, to embrace and love people who may not have a lot of this world's things, but are rich in their love, loyalty, and friendship. In short, those early days, when I was working hard and had little, really gave me the foundation for thriving and living a blessed life despite my circumstances. Like the apostle Paul, I learned to be content and thankful in every season, and not to base my attitude solely on how big my bank account was or what kind of a job I had at the time. God taught me that I could be happy and thankful in every situation, even as He was positioning me for future blessing and opportunities.

In mentoring people who are preparing for their careers and pursuing their God-given destinies, I always emphasize the importance of embracing and enjoying the seasons they are in at any given moment. God is in charge of your destiny, and He knows what you need to prepare you for the next chapter of your life. There are no circumstances or situations in which you find yourself that have to hold negative connotations or hold you back. If there is one thing I've learned, it is that God has a storehouse of joy for us in every season of life, no matter how difficult.

IF THERE IS ONE THING I'VE LEARNED, IT IS THAT GOD HAS A STOREHOUSE OF JOY FOR US IN EVERY SEASON OF LIFE, NO MATTER HOW DIFFICULT.

EVERY CHAPTER IS A BLESSING

Susan is right! Every chapter and season of your life, no matter how challenging and how much it stretches you, is worth embracing for the rich treasures that God has hidden there for your benefit. Just think about it. Look back on your life, from the good times and victories, to the mundane and ordinary, to those times during which you were struggling, went through some faith-deepening hardship, or were otherwise tried and tested by the winds of adversity. For me, at least, every one of those seasons came with a broad range of treasure for my future—things God taught me about myself, about His kingdom, and about how to walk in faith to see God's future goodness. And in addition He made certain that there were abundant memories and recollections of good times with my family, of how we made it through those times and were close, and how God kept us in the palm of His hand.

What is more, the chapters of my life where everything was clicking along nicely, where there were few trials or hardships to compete with the good times—the memories from those seasons are neither more sweet nor satisfying than the memories of the tough and lean times. In reality, God gives grace and mercy to see us through each circumstance, and His desire is for us to embrace every season with passion, joy, and an expectation of His mercy and goodness.

DON'T BE IN A HURRY!

If you are like me, when you were a child you couldn't wait to grow up, to see what life had in store for you, and to finally be able to do all the things that adults kept telling you were "too young" for. But now, looking back, many of us wish we could revisit being a kid, when life was simpler and excitement was easier. We wish, if only for a day, to go back to our years of school, friends, and family, to hear the reassuring voice of a mom, dad, or grandparent, and to shed the responsibilities, pressures, and limitations that come to us as adults.

Sadly, many adults embrace the same attitudes they had as kids, wishing to move on quickly to the next chapter of life—to leave behind things that may seem unpleasant, difficult, or just downright dull. How many of us have wanted to quit a tedious job or abandon an unpleasant responsibility, to move on to something more exciting and colorful? How many times have we coasted through some duty or commitment we were called on to perform, simply counting the days or hours until we were free?

But friend, for those of us into whom God has placed a destiny to fulfill—and yes, that includes *you*—we cannot afford to entertain such an attitude. Fulfilling our destiny requires of us a higher reach. I believe that, just as with Susan, we must embrace *every* season of our lives, and every day of every season, with passion and joy, considering each day a supreme gift from God. The apostle Paul counsels us that we are to face every day, every duty, every opportunity enthusiastically, as though we are responding personally to God, *"knowing that from the Lord [we] will receive the reward of the inheritance."*[1]

Every season of your life is a gift from your heavenly Father, who planned your destiny and has its unfolding in His hand. There is nothing that you should take for granted, as though some of your days, and some of your seasons, are less important than others. Friend, I do not think God considers any day of your life unimportant. Each has the potential for bearing the fruit of the Spirit!

YOU ONLY HAVE TODAY

The writer of Ecclesiastes put it this way, saying that in each season of life, "whatever your hand finds to do, do it with all of your might, because there will be no work or planning for the future, or any wisdom to perform anything, in the grave where each of us is going."[2] Of course, we know that here and now is the only time we have to reach our destiny, to bear fruit for eternity, and to have an influence

1. Colossians 3:24.
2. See Ecclesiastes 9:10.

on others for the kingdom of God. But how many of us still find ourselves wishing for a "new thing," or a "better opportunity"? Friend, here and now is your season of life! Yes, God may be positioning and preparing you for a new chapter in the days ahead. Maybe your full destiny is yet to be unfolded in all the glory God has planned, and tomorrow will bring a more exciting or new opportunity straight from God's throne. But I counsel you not to discount your *today* while waiting for your *tomorrow*.

Like Susan, you may find yourself in school or working hard to make ends meet as you anticipate a new season of life. Maybe you have faithfully and diligently served in some capacity in the marketplace, in ministry, or in a private concern, believing that God has you there to prune and prepare you for better, bigger, more exciting things. But now you are beginning to wonder if the effort and expectation has been worth it as days and months have turned into years—with no discernible change in your circumstances or prospects for a new chapter in life.

Friend, don't give up on the season you are in. I believe that God has indeed spoken life and prosperity to your future and destiny, and His timing is perfect. Just as in every other aspect of your life, in this area of God's destiny for you I encourage you not to "*cast away your confidence*" in what God has spoken deep in your heart, because He has promised that you will reap a great reward of His rich blessing if you hold fast.[3] God promises that in "*due season*" you will reap the reward, if you do not faint and give up in the process.[4]

A SEASON FOR EVERYTHING

The Word of God is clear that the heavenly Father created the seasons of our lives in the same way He designed the seasons that rule the earthly realm. It is crucial that we submit to each season so that we can reap the harvest that God has planned for us.

3. Hebrews 10:35–36.
4. Galatians 6:9.

I am sure you are familiar with the passage in Ecclesiastes that speaks of seasons. While one of the simplest passages in Scripture, it is also profound for the reality it brings to our hearts as we contemplate God's design. In it, we learn that to everything in our world *"there is a season, and a time to every purpose under the heaven."*

> *A time to be born, and a time to die; a time to plant, and a time to pluck up that which is planted;*
>
> *A time to kill, and a time to heal; a time to break down, and a time to build up;*
>
> *A time to weep, and a time to laugh; a time to mourn, and a time to dance;*
>
> *A time to cast away stones, and a time to gather stones together; a time to embrace, and a time to refrain from embracing;*
>
> *A time to get, and a time to lose; a time to keep, and a time to cast away;*
>
> *A time to rend, and a time to sew; a time to keep silence, and a time to speak;*
>
> *A time to love, and a time to hate; a time of war, and a time of peace.*[5]

Each of us will face a broad range of experiences in life. Just as we were born and came into this world with hope and purpose, whether we want to acknowledge it or not, it is certain that we will all also face the end of our lives someday. Each of us will face both times of laughter and joy, as well as our share of weeping, sadness, and heartache.

Without Jesus as the anchor of our lives, these truths would leave us hopeless and discouraged. If we are all going to face pain, tears, heartache, and, ultimately, death, what is the point of life? The good news, of course, is that as God's children, all the seasons of our lives are leading us to a rich and fruitful destiny in this life, and an eternity

---

5. Ecclesiastes 3:1–8 KJV.

of glorious life in the joyous presence of our Lord and Savior Jesus Christ.

Yes, each of us will face seasons of trial and hardship, but God also has a rich purpose for us as we trust in Him daily in each season of life. As for the difficult seasons, God's Word assures us that His favor over us will bring us life, and though for a night season we may face tears, the joy of God's best for us will break through in the morning.[6]

Dear child of God, each season you face—from the difficult and challenging to the most hopeful and exciting—is meant to guide you to God's very best blessings. You have a destiny to fulfill, through each chapter and phase God places before you, and although a particular season may seem to drag on longer than you would like, take heart. The prophet Habakkuk assures us that God's purpose will come to pass: *"though it tarry, wait for it; because it will surely come."*[7]

The seasons of your life, determined by your heavenly Father, are as certain as the seasons that rule this earth. Genesis 8:22 tells us that from the beginning of creation God determined that *"while the earth remains, seedtime and harvest, cold and heat, summer and winter, and day and night shall not cease."* The farmer working his field knows this, and even though he may feel impatient for the growing season to end and make way for the abundant harvest he expects to reap, he knows that he must wait for the season to conclude.

In the same way, God has determined your times and seasons, and though you may be tempted to grow impatient in the process of living through any particular season, be assured that God has a rich harvest of destiny for you. Each season of your life will run its course and make way for the next beautiful chapter. Just as every season in our natural world—from spring and summer to autumn and winter—has its own special beauty and purpose in God's design, so every season in your life has specific significance in God's purpose for you. Friend,

---

6. See Psalm 30:5.
7. Habakkuk 2:3 KJV.

allow God to have His way in your life, so that you can reap the entire, perfect harvest He has for you and lack no good thing.[8]

In His time, as each season passes, He will make everything in your life beautiful and complete, and with the psalmist you can confidently declare over your life: *"The LORD will perfect that which concerns me."*[9]

---

8. See James 1:4.
9. Psalm 138:8.

STRESS NEVER BRINGS SUCCESS,
BUT RESTING ALWAYS BRINGS BLESSING.

FAVOR
TAKEAWAY

17

UNLESS THE LORD BUILD THE HOUSE...

Throughout the pages of this book we have been discussing your destiny—acknowledging the fact that God has an exclusive one just for you, unique, awesome, and filled with blessing and abundance. We have seen that His desire for you to reach your specific, divinely created destiny and purpose is even greater than your own desire to receive it.

Throughout the ages of time, God has had a unique place and purpose for every person who has walked the earth. But there are more people who miss that destiny than those who reach it—although, as we have seen, entering God's destiny is not complicated. Why is it that so many people miss their calling and purpose in life? Why is it that even many of God's own children, with unlimited access to His Word and the counsel of the Holy Spirit, too often stumble blindly through years of missteps and disappointment rather than stepping into all that God has freely prepared for them to enjoy? I believe it is because they are relying on their own strength and understanding to chart their course, rather than completely placing their destiny and future in God's hands and walking out the seasons of life in His strength and wisdom. What we really need is faith and obedience.

"THERE IS A WAY THAT SEEMS RIGHT..."

The influence, advice, and example of others can provide a powerful incentive to move in a direction that seems good but is not God's perfect will. The Bible tells us that there is a way that may seem right, but ultimately it leads to heartache and the destruction of our God-birthed dreams.[1] How many individuals have we witnessed who start out well but finish poorly? They give their heart and life to Jesus, with plans to serve and obey Him, but as the months and years go by, the clamor of this world begins to replace the quiet and steady direction God provides through His Word and His Spirit. Music, movies, television, and casual conversation carry the message of the prevailing culture and can have a subtle, but powerful, influence on God's people, drowning out faith and destroying the best of intentions if not challenged with the truth of God's Word.

Similarly, if not filtered through God's Word and prayer, the advice of friends, family, and others can turn us down a path that will take us away from God's best for our lives. Worldly advice about career, finances, relationships, and family can sound convincing—even if it is diametrically opposed to the kingdom of God—if we don't have the sure foundation of God's Word to guide us.

ROCK OR SAND?

King Solomon, considered the wisest man who ever lived, said that unless the Lord is in charge of what we are building in this life, all of our planning and efforts will be in vain because what we construct will be built on a weak foundation.[2] Jesus offered a valuable parable about the importance of our life's foundation being laid on God's eternal principles. He told a story about two men who each built a house, one constructing his on rock, the other on sand. Now both houses no doubt were built with the best materials available, and were beautiful, stable-looking structures. As long as their surroundings remained

1. See Proverbs 14:12.
2. See Psalm 127:1.

calm and untroubled, both men were safe and secure in their homes. But when the inevitable winds, rains, and floods tore through the land, only one house remained standing. Jesus said that when the severe elements assaulted the wise man's house, it stood firm with no danger of falling because *"it was founded upon a rock."* However, when the severe weather came and beat with all its fury on the foolish man's house, it tumbled down, because it was built on shifting, uncertain sand. *"And great was the fall"* of that house, said Jesus.[3]

Friend, as a child of God, saved through the blood of Jesus Christ, you have the opportunity to make the foundation of your future, destiny, and purpose strong and secure. Yes, it is good, right, and proper for you to pursue education, to desire a career, to plan passionately for your future. God wants you to prosper in everything to which you set your hand, and He is clear that the wise person plans for his or her future endeavors.[4] But as Solomon said, with all your planning, pursuing, and getting, make absolutely certain that the main thing you get is God's wisdom and understanding, because it provides the solid rock foundation for everything else.[5]

THE ONLY CERTAINTY WE HAVE IS STANDING ON THE ROCK OF CHRIST AND UNDER THE SHADOW OF HIS PROTECTION.

More than ever before we live in uncertain times. The world is in turmoil, the economy tenuous, and even the circumstances of our own lives and families can seem unsettled. Friend, the only certainty we have is standing on the rock of Christ and under the shadow of His

3. Matthew 7:24–27 kjv.
4. See Proverbs 21:20.
5. See, for example, Proverbs 4:7.

protection. He has promised that for His people there is no reason to fear, for He will make our way sure. We must not allow our plans to be born out of worldly wisdom. The only true wisdom and understanding for us lies in God's Word.

THE EXAMPLE OF SOLOMON

Ironically, the life of Solomon offers us a compelling example of the importance of seeking God and His wisdom in all we do and the tragic consequences of allowing the influence of this world to divert us from God's best.

Remember that Solomon had the advantage of being the son of Israel's greatest king, David, whom God called a man after His own heart. From the very beginning of his life, Solomon was no doubt mentored and trained up in the ways of God, for his divine destiny was to follow David on the throne, lead God's people Israel, and build the temple that God had placed in David's heart to build.

Scripture recounts that when the time came for Solomon to step into his destiny as the king of Israel, he made a monumental choice that dramatically impacted the direction his life and legacy took. Coming to Solomon one night in a dream, God presented the young king with an incredible offer. "Ask!" God said to Solomon. "What shall I give you?"[6]

Amazingly, God was handing Solomon a blank check with the offer to fill in what Solomon would like to have: riches, long life, military conquest of all his enemies. Solomon could have had anything his heart desired. But what this young, inexperienced king with his life ahead of him asked for instead was wisdom, understanding, and discernment, to know God's direction in all of his endeavors.

"God, you have given me oversight of Your people," Solomon told the Lord. "But I am like a little child who does not know his way. Give

---

6. See 1 Kings 3:5–14.

me eyes to see, Lord, a heart to understand, and a spirit that will know how to govern your people rightly."

In essence, God had placed a test before Solomon, to see how he would respond at this critical early juncture of his career. And God was well-pleased with Solomon's response. "Because you didn't ask selfishly for riches or other things that might have served your personal ambition, but instead asked for the highest treasure possible—My divine wisdom—here is what I am going to do," God told Solomon. "I am going to give it all to you. First, You will go down in history as the wisest and most discerning king who ever lived. I will pour into you the secrets of My kingdom so that you will be divinely empowered to steward My most precious possession, My people Israel."

Then God added a clause that resounded with His glory and power: "I will also give you what you did not ask for—riches and honor—so that there shall not be any king or ruler throughout the earth like unto you all of your days."

Finally, God concluded by promising Solomon that "if you will walk in My ways, to keep my statutes and commandments just like your father David did, then I will make your life long on the earth."

A TRAGIC TALE

What befell Solomon and the generations that followed him is a tragic tale. Solomon did, indeed, rule with wisdom and discernment, and under his administration Israel enjoyed its most prosperous era. Solomon was known as a master builder, and throughout his reign not only was Israel's first temple constructed—a massive and beautiful edifice dedicated to worshipping God— but Solomon oversaw many construction projects that raised Israel's stature as a nation. Second Chronicles 8 indicates that whatever Solomon put his hand to in the way of municipal and construction projects prospered and succeeded.

Similarly, his wealth was beyond compare, and the military might that Israel wielded under Solomon was such that few nations challenged this people blessed by God. Second Chronicles 9:22–23 says that King Solomon was greater in both riches and wisdom than any other leader on earth, and the whole world came to him seeking to hear the knowledge that God had placed within his heart. Through Solomon, God was fulfilling the promise that He had made generations before when the children of Israel first entered the Promised Land to claim their inheritance. Under a fully submitted, humble, and committed man of God, Israel flourished and prospered mightily.

But then something happened. In the middle of all this prosperity and success Solomon took his eyes off the Source of his blessings and turned to what the world had to offer. Of course, it didn't happen overnight, but subtly, over a period of years, Solomon was seduced by the gods, philosophies, and principles of the world.

First of all, Scripture recounts that Solomon began to love *"many foreign women"* who did not know or fear God and who succeeded in turning Solomon's heart away from following after the Lord.[7] Amazingly, the Bible tells us that Solomon amassed for his own pleasure and passion a total of seven hundred wives and three hundred other lovers or concubines.

Living in his enormous mansion, with his horses, chariots, gold, and other possessions, and the clamor of his hundreds of wives and concubines buzzing around him, Solomon began to lose the sensitivity he once had to the voice of the Lord, as other voices competed for his attention. With the increase of possessions, influence, and abundance, Solomon no doubt began to assume that, after all, it was his own wisdom, efforts, and strength that had made him so successful. The warning from Israel's prophets both past and present, that Solomon and the nation of Israel must not forget their God and His Word, increasingly fell on deaf ears. And so began Solomon's slow, tragic descent from the glory and destiny for which God had created him—and so began the ultimate destruction of the nation of Israel.

---

7. 1 Kings 11:1.

After Solomon's death, his son Rehoboam took the throne, and it soon became apparent that he possessed none of the God-given wisdom of his father, or the mercy and meekness of his grandfather David. Instead of treating the people of Israel with mercy and kindness, as the older men of Israel who had stood with Solomon counseled him, Rehoboam took the wicked advice of the younger men with little experience and less wisdom, who counseled Rehoboam to oppress his subjects and treat them with contempt—to "show them who's boss."

That advice spelled the beginning of the end for Rehoboam and the kingdom of Israel, as ten of the twelve tribes rebelled against him, and the nation of Israel was split in two. For the next several hundred years, the ten tribes of Israel remained at enmity with their brethren, the two tribes of Judah and Benjamin, as a succession of both good and wicked kings struggled to maintain two kingdoms that had lost the unblemished blessing and favor of God.

Finally, in 722 BC, the ten tribes of Israel were conquered and destroyed by the Assyrians, followed by the destruction of Judah in 586 BC, when Solomon's beautiful temple was sacked and destroyed and many of the children of Israel were exiled to Babylon. It would take another forty-plus years before God allowed His deeply humbled people to return to their homeland.

FEAR GOD, FOLLOW HIS WAYS

It didn't have to end this way. The counsel of Scripture makes it clear that God had a much different plan for Solomon and for the nation of Israel. God's plan was for a future and a hope for His people, which would come through committing their way to Him and trusting Him wholly and implicitly. Even as they rebelled over and over against His ways throughout the centuries, God was ever faithful, ready to forgive, heal, and guide them.

Many scholars speculate that shortly before his death, but after so much damage had been done spiritually to Israel, Solomon returned to the God of his youth. Whatever the case, it is clear that he realized he had strayed from God's "master blueprint." Looking back on his life with its wisdom, wealth, and conquests, and with all the heartache that went with it, Solomon wrote: *"Now all has been heard; here is the conclusion of the matter: fear God and keep his commandments, for this is the duty of all mankind."*[8]

THE PATH TO GREATNESS

The apostle Paul tells us that the examples we see in Scripture are given to us so that we will know how to conduct our own lives—how to trust God, follow His plan, and see the greatness and destiny He has for us come to pass.[9] So what is it that we can learn from the example of Solomon and the nation of Israel? Clearly it is that if we wish to walk in the full destiny that God has for us, we must allow Him to "build the house" He has for each of us. Every effort we put forth that is not founded on His Word and principles will be in vain.

In my own life, as I have pursued excellence and God's best for my life, I have found four foundational principles that have helped me immensely to stay on track, to keep my bearings in His way, and to grow in God's greatness for me. I believe that these four simple principles will also help you to keep your compass true to God's direction in your life.

WHATEVER IT IS YOUR HAND FINDS TO DO IN THIS LIFE, DO IT WITH ALL OF YOUR HEART, SOUL, AND STRENGTH.

8. Ecclesiastes 12:13 NIV.
9. See1 Corinthians 10:6, 11.

THE FIRST PRINCIPLE: POSSESS PASSION

Friend, you only have one life in which to fulfill God's purpose for you, and if you want to hit the mark, a passion for what you are pursuing is key. What do I mean by passion? Some see passion as a "white hot" intensity that drives a person obsessively and aggressively to pursue whatever it is he or she is "passionate" about, be it fishing, cooking, football, career, relationships—or Jesus. But that kind of thinking is not passion. That's nothing more than a recipe for a burned-out lifestyle.

Instead, passion is all about maintaining a steady vision that will guide you to your expected end, to the place and purpose God has for you. True passion, you see, is really an immovable determination to live your life in such a way that when you leave this earth you will be used up, having fulfilled all that God destined you to do. The last thing you want as a child of God—with all the treasure of His kingdom at your disposal—is to come to the end of your life and fill the grave with your potential. Friend, I challenge you to live your life so that at the end of it all your grave will be empty save for the shell of your used-up body. When your friends and family gaze at your final resting place, they will be able to confidently say of you the same thing they said of Jesus: He is not here. He is risen!

As a child of God, true passion begins with your pursuit of God. In Psalm 63:8, King David says to God: *"My soul follows close behind You."* That is true passion for what really matters in life. Earlier in the same chapter David writes that His soul *"thirsts"* for God, *"my flesh longs for You in a dry and thirsty land."*[10]

The apostle Paul also addresses the issue of passion, admonishing that *"Whatever you do, work at it with all your heart, as working for the Lord, not for human masters."*[11] You see, passion begins right where you are, first in steadily, consistently, daily seeking to love and live for the Lord. As you move down that road God will spark the passion for

10. Psalm 63:1.
11. Colossians 3:23 NIV.

your specific purpose in life. Too many people live their lives always looking to the future, thinking that their destiny will start tomorrow, or the next day, or when a certain set of circumstances and successes line up.

But that is not how God's plan works. Your destiny begins with being passionate and purposeful about what He has placed in front of you today. Maybe that is a job you don't particularly care for, or a set of college courses that you find tedious and boring. Maybe it is faithfully serving in some small capacity in your church, even though you don't feel particularly called or inspired in that position. The examples are endless, but the principle is the same: passion begins and ends with faithfulness in that to which God has called you right now, even as you pray, prepare, and pursue a God-inspired dream and destiny that transcends your present circumstances.

PASSION BEGINS AND ENDS WITH FAITHFULNESS.

THE SECOND PRINCIPLE: EMBRACE FAITH

Scripture is clear that without faith it is impossible to step into the realm of God's greatness and destiny for you, because *"he who comes to God must believe that He is, and that He is a rewarder of those who diligently seek Him."*[12]

Now listen! Diligence speaks to the principle of faith! Do you want God's best? Do you want to walk in that place of power, purpose, confidence, and authority that will illuminate and energize your

---

12. Hebrews 11:6.

realm of influence? Then diligence to take hold of God, of His purposes, and of unwavering faith is absolutely essential.

Many individuals think that only those with "great" faith can step out and believe God to take them into the realm of the impossible. But Jesus said that even with "mustard seed" faith, as small as to be nearly undiscernible to the average person, you can move the mountains that block your destiny.

And the great thing about faith is that, the more you use it, the stronger it becomes in your life. My counsel to all who are passionately pursuing God's best is this: Ask God to increase your faith. Ask Him to place you in situations and circumstances that will incrementally challenge you to new levels of trusting God for the impossible. Believe me, in the days to come God is going to increasingly look for men and women who can step out in faith—with no "Plan B" available to them. These are the ones who will step into the choicest places of God's kingdom advance. Friend, sign up right now for that training ground, and walk each day with a prayer on your lips for God to move you into the realm of miracles and the impossible!

THE THIRD PRINCIPLE: CONFRONT YOUR CHALLENGES

While the world teaches us to hide and disguise our weaknesses, shortcomings, and needs, the truth is that even the most successful of individuals must come to terms with issues that threaten to short-circuit their destiny. For the godly businessman it may be a severe lack of funds to compete in the marketplace. For the student with a call to law, education, ministry, or business, it may be difficult classes that threaten his or her future and success. For many individuals, the challenges may be internal—a lack of confidence, a sense of inferiority, or the past criticism of others—that hold them back and threaten their destiny. For others it may `be a past sin or long-ago misstep that the enemy continues to use to convince them that they have been disqualified from greatness, and must settle for second best.

I love the story of Nick Vujicic, a young man who was born without arms or legs. Not surprisingly, while Nick was raised in a home with loving parents who supported him and encouraged him to look past his enormous limitations, he nonetheless struggled throughout his childhood with why God had created him differently from others. He battled depression and loneliness and he wondered whether he even had a purpose in life. But just as He does in each of our lives, God reached down and touched this young man, assured him that he did, indeed, have a destiny and calling, and that he was meant for greatness.

As Nick focused on the One who called and equipped him, and took his eyes off the challenges, he began to flourish in his purpose. Today Nick travels the world and tells people about the love of God, their purpose in Christ, and how they can surmount all the challenges that confront them and be successful through God's fullness in their lives. "If God can use a man without arms and legs to be His hands and feet," says Nick, "then He will certainly use any willing heart!"[13]

What are the challenges that confront you and threaten your future and destiny in Christ? You can—and will—be victorious over every obstacle with faith, perseverance, and God's Spirit working in you.

In fact, God emphasizes that He is most effective in the lives of those who are convinced of their own weakness and inability to succeed alone. Remember: when you are weak, He is strong.[14]

THE FOURTH PRINCIPLE: PREPARE FOR SUCCESS

There is an old proverb that goes: "Those who fail to prepare are preparing to fail." That saying reminds me of the story about a young man in school who noticed that the young lady sitting in the desk in front of him always got straight As on all of her assignments and tests. "What's the secret?" he asked her one day. "You always do so well in

---

13. Nick Vujicic, "Bio," LifeWithoutLimbs.org, http://www.lifewithoutlimbs.org/about-nick/bio/ (accessed March 3, 2017).
14. See 2 Corinthians 12:10.

school, while it seems I'm always failing a test or getting bad grades on my assignments."

The young lady thought a moment, then said, "Well, I always pray and ask God to help me with my school work, and to do well, and He's never failed me yet. Why don't you pray? God is no respecter of persons."

There was a big test in class the next day, and the young man took his friend's advice to heart, praying fervently that night that God would help him do well in the morning. A few days later, however, the young man was shocked and disconcerted when the test results came back—and he had failed the exam miserably. The young lady, however, had gotten a perfect score.

"I guess God just didn't hear my prayer," the young man said dejectedly. "I prayed hard, but look at my test."

"Maybe you just need to put a little more effort into studying," the girl suggested. "How much time did you spend preparing for the test?"

The young man hung his head a bit and had to admit that he hadn't studied at all for the test. "I thought you meant that prayer was enough."

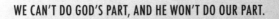

WE CAN'T DO GOD'S PART, AND HE WON'T DO OUR PART.

Friend, that attitude is all too common among believers today. Many Christians think that God is simply standing by, waiting until the time is just right to hand them success and a rich destiny, with little or no effort on their part. But the truth is far different. If you desire to enter into all the best that God has to offer, you must prepare to walk through the doors He is indicating for you. I have often said: We can't do God's part, and He WON'T do our part.

You cannot fulfill the destiny God has created you for if you have not prepared and positioned yourself for success. Please hear me well in this important aspect of reaching your place and purpose in life. God's call to you is an invitation to join Him in the glorious advance of His kingdom. Be assured that He will open all the doors that are necessary for you to step into the destiny He has for you in His kingdom—the role He created just for you. But that invitation requires a response on your part. Has God called you to a profession in education, business, the law, medicine, or media? All of those callings require training, education, and mentorship. And that means applying yourself to study, learning, and growing through hard work and preparation.

Recall that when the apostle Paul was mentoring the young Timothy, a pastor and apostle in training, he counseled him: "Study to show yourself approved, a workman who does not need to be ashamed."[15] You see, God had, indeed, called Timothy to a position of leadership and ministry. But that call was, in effect, an invitation for Timothy to enter the training cycle that would be necessary for him to succeed in ministry. Had Timothy not heeded Paul's counsel he would have had no message to preach, no power and impact for ministry.

Dear child of God, your responsibility is clear: ask God to show you the path of preparation that will be necessary for you to reach the next level of God's plan for you. That preparation may be schooling, a time of mentorship, and a period of hiddenness as God molds and makes you into His person. It will most certainly mean growing in the Word of God and prayer—a training ground that will last your entire life.

---

15. 2 Timothy 2:15, author's paraphrase.

YOUR TRAINING GROUND FOR DESTINY

Think of the path of such men and women of God in Scripture as Abraham, Moses, Joshua, David, Esther, Daniel, Peter, Paul, and many others. Each of these great servants of the Most High spent years in preparation, testing, trials, and learning before they stepped onto the stage of God's historic timetable.

And how about our own Savior and Lord? Consider that Jesus Himself was hidden in preparation for thirty long years leading up to the three short years of ministry that culminated in the fulfillment of His destiny: His monumental suffering and death, followed by His miraculous resurrection.

Jesus is our example, who, even though He was the perfect Son of God, submitted to the earthly path of preparation so that we would have a pattern to follow. Friend, if you are waiting for the next step in the unfolding of your destiny, consider yourself to be in an important time of preparation, and ask God to empower you with the necessary faith, confidence, and perseverance to successfully pass this time of training.

Remember, it is essential that God be at the very foundation of your plans and preparation. Spending time in His Word, communing with Him in prayer, and asking for His guidance will ensure that you stay on the path that leads to your destiny. Then, as you take the necessary steps in the natural, through schooling, mentorship, practice, and other preparation, you will find yourself passing sign posts and milestones that will give you assurance that you are on the right road—the road that God had chosen for you even before you were born.

You will be able to declare with the apostle Paul that *"He who has begun a good work in you will complete it"*[16]—right up until that day when you step into His presence to be with Him for all eternity.

---

16. Philippians 1:6.

A PRAYER FOR YOUR DESTINY

Allow me to close this book with a prayer of faith that God will, indeed, complete the good work He started in you, bringing you to your desire and destiny:

Dear Heavenly Father,

You have promised to give us all that we need to fulfill Your purpose in our lives. I thank You right now for what you are doing in the life of this your child and the one to whom You have promised a destiny and inheritance.

I call forth wisdom, discernment, and direction into their life. Make clear the path you have for this Your child. Place before them the opportunity, the people, the favor, the divine appointments that will make their road straight. Give them a supernatural abundance of perseverance and determination to walk through the hard times and each season that is necessary to fulfill their destiny.

Fill this precious child of Yours with an abundance of faith to believe, even against impossible circumstances, that they will succeed and reach that place of destiny and purpose to which You have called them. Teach and empower them to call those things that are not as though they were, and to expect to see the goodness of the Lord in the here and now.

Father, You are good and faithful all the time, and I commit this precious child of Yours into Your hands of provision and perfection—in the name of Jesus, Amen.

ABOUT THE AUTHOR

Bishop Henry B. Fernandez, inspirational speaker, author, and entrepreneur, is known worldwide for his practical, dynamic Bible teaching, and powerful, prophetic preaching that cuts across denominational, cultural, and economic barriers. Bishop Fernandez is senior pastor of the Faith Center Ministries—a thriving, multiracial congregation of over ten thousand in Fort Lauderdale, Florida.

Bishop Fernandez is a visionary and challenging leader who believes it is God's will for every believer to walk in prosperity and divine health. He is committed to helping educate people to what God's Word has to say about living and walking in victory. Part of that commitment is demonstrated through his founding of the University of Fort Lauderdale, a nondenominational Christian institute fully approved by the Commission for Independent Education. The university, which was established to advance Christian education and promote leadership in both secular and faith-based areas, offers degrees at the associate, bachelor, master, and doctoral levels.

His wife, Carol Fernandez, serves as co-pastor of the Faith Center Ministries and often ministers alongside him at conferences as well as in their home church. They are the parents of two sons, Seion-Zane and Elijah-Zane.